"Leslie is an expert on creating deeply meaningful and transformative garden spaces. This delightful book is equal parts inspiring and instructive. It's brimming with ideas, whether you want to fill your plot with food or flowers."

—ERIN BENZAKEIN, owner of Floret Farm and *New York Times* bestselling author of *Floret Farm's A Year in Flowers*

"*Garden Wonderland* is a wonderful exploration of garden design, beauty, and nourishment all firmly rooted in a deep respect for the diversity of nature and human culture. The book inspires and instructs us on how to design gardens of profound fullness, sustained by powerful values of connection, family, community, and care. Through story and imagery, *Garden Wonderland* reminds us that plants should be part of everyday for everyone: as food, experience, deep memory, and creativity."

—JENNIFER JEWELL, creator and host of the *Cultivating Place* public radio program and podcast, and author of *What We Sow*

"Whether you're an experienced gardener or embarking on this journey for the first time, *Garden Wonderland* serves as a guide through the transformative process of designing, cultivating, and wholeheartedly embracing your distinct outdoor haven. Leslie Bennett, a renowned landscape designer and visionary, along with writer and editor Julie Chai, fervently convey how a garden, when infused with purpose, evolves into a sanctuary of breathtaking beauty, a reflection of personal heritage, and a limitless wellspring of creativity."

—BRYANT TERRY, chef, James Beard and NAACP Image award–winning author of *Black Food* and editor in chief of 4 Color Books

garden
wonderland

garden *wonder*land

CREATE LIFE-CHANGING
OUTDOOR SPACES FOR BEAUTY,
HARVEST, MEANING, AND JOY

Leslie Bennett
and Julie Chai

PHOTOGRAPHS BY RACHEL WEILL

TEN SPEED PRESS
California | New York

'Lavender Lady' mangave

Contents

Introduction   1

PART I *How-To*

one
What is a garden wonderland?
7

two
Create a garden that works for you
15

three
Use plants for form, function, and delight
33

PART II *Inspiration*

four
Edible wonderlands
57

five
Floral wonderlands
99

six
Healing wonderlands
131

seven
Gathering wonderlands
161

eight
Cultural wonderlands
213

Gratitude   256
Garden design credits   258
About the contributors   259
Index   260

Introduction

A garden can be so much more than a backyard sitting area or a place with plants in the ground. Many of us think of our outdoor spaces in the simplest of terms—such as low-maintenance, native, flower, or veggie gardens—that have been popularized by magazines and makeover shows. But these skip over a garden's true potential for impacting our lives for the better. In fact, with a little intention our gardens can be shaped into what I think of as real-life wonderlands—that is, places where we can grow our relationship with plants, experience awe-inspiring beauty, attune with nature and the seasons, and integrate a sense of abundance that inspires creativity and sharing—all while remembering and choosing the stories we tell about who we are and how we belong.

Simply put, our gardens can be where we find more connected, inspired, and grounded versions of ourselves. In my own backyard, I'm surrounded by plants that show off my favorite colors, scents, and flavors and that connect to my childhood memories and heritage. It's a backyard created with intention and that makes room for the experiences—both simple and profound—that I want to have in my life. In my garden wonderland I have the opportunity to marvel at a flock of birds on my persimmon tree, feel thrilled by the shifting colors of a rose in bloom, or enjoy the fragrance of angel's trumpet on a summer evening with friends. I may pass fall-harvested quince over the fence to my neighbor so he can make his favorite membrillo (quince paste) recipe to share with me, or build a fort with my kids using banana leaves, like their father and grandfather used to do in their own rural Jamaican childhoods.

I know from experience in my own garden, and those of my clients, that the relationships we develop with the land and with the plants we grow in our gardens can truly enrich our lives. I believe these bonds and support are things we all can, and have a right to, experience. My intention in this book is to provide guidance and inspiration that invite you to shape your own available outdoor areas into personal garden wonderlands that will nurture and help you grow the world you want to live in for yourself, your loved ones, and your community.

OPPOSITE My family's backyard is a lush, dynamic space to grow, harvest, and relax in all year. Here, my children and I sample the summer harvest.

My view of wonderland

I've always loved plants and felt connected to the natural landscapes I grew up with in California's Bay Area. But early on, I didn't consider a career that would put me in direct contact with plants or the land. Instead, as the daughter of English and Jamaican immigrants who encouraged me to pursue a more traditional profession, I found a compromise by earning an undergraduate degree in environmental justice, then went to law school. Focusing on land use and landscape preservation law, I experienced through my work that how we interact with the land, or don't, can dramatically impact our sense of self and the way we move through the world. It got me thinking, too, about the places where we have the greatest opportunity to interact with the land—which is often in our own yards. This solidified for me that how we choose to design and live with our gardens matters and was something I could dedicate myself to.

Inspired to explore my relationship with plants and land more deeply, I embarked on a life-changing apprenticeship on an organic farm during a break from work. Learning to grow food was such a profound experience that I felt in my gut it was something I needed to pursue fully. I took a leap of faith, trading my law career in New York City and London for a new way of life that had me covered in soil and surrounded by plants, and I've never looked back.

OPPOSITE, LEFT Green beans are a fun, easy-to-grow summer crop that my kids love to pick.

OPPOSITE, RIGHT Angel's trumpet (*Brugmansia* 'Charles Grimaldi') blooms bring warm color to the garden and offer evening fragrance.

THIS PAGE Our garden includes fruit for every season; pluots are ready in July.

African blue basil and variegated scented geranium (*Pelargonium*) are my go-to foliage for fragrant from-the-garden arrangements. A few blooms—Lady of Shallot rose, blue cornflower, yarrow, and *Trachelium caeruleum* 'Hamer Pandora'—add color.

While working at farms and gardens on my ancestral lands of rural England and Jamaica and in my home state of California, I learned that it was possible to grow an astounding amount of food in a home garden–sized space and that creating beauty with plants was deeply impactful to everyone who experienced it. I also discovered that I had instinctual knowledge about how to grow things, as I believe we all do.

Gardens are for all of us

I have since founded Pine House Edible Gardens, a landscape design and build firm based in Oakland, California. After more than fifteen years of garden designing and tending, I've learned so much about how to make gardens that truly support our lives—mostly through trial and error and by surrounding myself with people I can learn from. In my work and travels, I've seen firsthand the wide-ranging, creative ways people make and connect with their gardens. I've learned that achieving a landscape that you can nurture, and that nurtures you in return, is about using plants to support an immersive experience where inspiration, connection, belonging, and new ways of being can unfold.

In this book

I am forever thankful to writer-editor Julie Chai for partnering with me on this book project and helping me to share my vision with you. In the pages ahead, you'll learn my approach for creating your own garden wonderland, from big-picture concepts to more step-by-step tasks. You'll also read about a series of gardens created by the amazing Pine House team of landscape designers and architects past and present, especially Holly Kuljian, Lonna Lopez, and Jessica Comerford. Whether a tiny backyard plot or an estate, each project has a different emphasis, reflecting the things that matter most to the homeowners and inviting you to see our design process coming to life. Together, these wonderlands show a broad perspective of how people are finding their connections, and themselves, in their front and backyards and offer views of how gardens can be as meaningful and unique as each of us. You'll see how life changing these gardens are and how you can achieve this for yourself too.

Leslie

one

What is a garden wonderland?

Each person's wonderland will of course be different, as what feeds our individual spirits is as diverse as we are. What nurtures you may be a food-filled plot, a garden with overflowing flowers, a place to commune with loved ones, a healing sanctuary, or something else. Whatever your focus as you approach your own space, I believe the aim of your design should be to create possibilities for experience, beauty, connection, and belonging. These are broad principles, so I'll start by explaining what they are and how to think generally about designing for them in your own outdoor area.

As you get started, this is a good time to get out a blank notepad so you can jot down ideas and goals and make sketches of anything you feel inspired to include as you read along.

OPPOSITE 'North Shore' and 'Triple G' sweet peas climb over an arched trellis for an inspired walk-through experience.

Breadseed poppy (*Papaver somniferum*) seed heads are beautiful in their own right and provide edible seed.

Farfugium japonicum, Trachelium caeruleum 'Hamer Pandora', and *Pittosporum tenuifolium* 'Marjorie Channon' are planted to maximize visual contrast.

Principle 1: Make plants part of your daily life

I believe in plant-centric gardens and that we are intended to live in relationship with the natural world, but we are often disconnected from truly experiencing that in our modern lives. Because the basis for any strong relationship is regular, ongoing, positive contact, creating a space that offers diverse, rich, spontaneous, and supportive daily experiences with plants is key. Your yard is one of the best and most available places for this.

Focusing on plants in a landscape may sound obvious, but so many of today's yards seem to center around expensive hardscape elements, an outdoor kitchen, or designer furniture. In contrast, a garden wonderland is a plant-based space where fairly minimal hardscape will do. By designing your garden using lots of lushly layered, interactive plants, you can create a place where you will be surrounded by plant and animal life and awaken all your senses. You may brush past a scented geranium and welcome its fragrance or savor the taste of luscious homegrown fruit. Your garden may inspire specific feelings, such as the awe of watching a butterfly visit the flowers you've planted, the pure relaxation brought on by wiggling your toes in the grass, the awareness of autumn brought on by changing leaves, or the delight of sharing the space with others.

OPPOSITE A simple gravel pathway lined with fragrant, edible English lavender, an apricot tree, and pineapple guava (*Feijoa sellowiana*) shrubs is beautiful and productive. Mountain cabbage tree (*Cussonia paniculata*) at the far end of the patio echoes the gray-green foliage of the lavender and pineapple guava but has an eye-catching, and contrasting, foliage shape.

Principle 2: Surround yourself with beauty

It's easy to speed through our days without pausing. But by deliberately surrounding ourselves with what we consider beautiful, we're gifting ourselves opportunities to stop and focus on things that invite wonder, gratitude, and awe and to let that beauty become part of our being.

Beauty is often presented as though it's a privilege of the rich and comfortable and even wasteful or frivolous to focus on if you're working with a smaller budget or are trying to make conscientious choices. None of this is true—we all have a birthright to be in connection with beauty, and you can choose to claim that any and every day.

A garden provides a special opportunity to collaborate with nature and co-create beauty, as we choose to include specific plants and arrange them to highlight the appeal of each. Especially if we're working in a limited space, we may feel conflicted about making room for what's most useful (such as edibles or a needed storage area) versus what's most visually pleasing. Remember that it's OK to prioritize what's beautiful as that's often what feeds our souls.

Lastly, remember that surrounding ourselves with beauty in a garden is a constant practice, as plants grow and change just as we do. By paying attention to how our landscape is evolving and adjusting as needed so that everything continues to work together and inspire, we give the greatest gift of care to ourselves and our communities.

Principle 3: Make space for connection

I believe—and have found to be true from the hundreds of gardens that the Pine House team and I have created over the years—that harvesting directly from your yard is one of the easiest and most powerful ways to remind you of your connection to the environment, other people, and yourself. In every garden we create, we include fruit, vegetables, culinary herbs, cutting flowers, and medicinal plants, all of which help highlight these connections. By tending the plants that feed and inspire us, we experience a reciprocal relationship through which we can learn how best to appreciate the land that we live with and harvest from each day.

OPPOSITE, LEFT Strawberries are an easy and delightful garden harvest.

OPPOSITE, RIGHT *Verbena bonariensis* attracts swallowtail butterflies and other pollinators to the garden.

The more you grow, the more opportunities for connection take root. Add plants and watch how many birds, bees, and all kinds of animal and insect life show up! As you spot more of these new critters in your garden, you may be prompted to learn about growing milkweed to support monarch butterflies, or find yourself simply setting aside time to sit and observe the birds that visit each day.

Whether you grow a few potted flowers or dedicate your entire yard to food production, growing plants in your garden wonderland is less about self-sufficiency and more about generating the abundance and creativity that will help you to connect to the people around you—sharing bumper crops with neighbors, using seasonal harvests to create new family recipes, or gifting a simple posy of freshly cut blooms.

Lastly, growing plants for harvest requires people, in this case—you! Humans have historically had a mutually beneficial relationship with the plants they're cultivating for food, shelter, medicine, and beauty. By tending to plants that nourish your own body and spirit, you become more present and connected to yourself.

Principle 4: Fortify your sense of belonging

Belonging is a natural human desire. One of the ways that we know we belong is by telling stories that remind us where we come from, who our family or community is, what we do, and even how we'd like to shape our future. We all descend from ancestors who used plants for food, shelter, medicine, and art, so our gardens and the plants in them can serve as conduits for returning to plant-based practices, rituals, and ways of being that we can make our own.

For many people, specific foods are very important reminders of their belonging. You can grow and eat food that links you with your family stories or cultural heritage. Beyond food, you can nurture other types of plants that are meaningful to you. This could mean planting medicinal lemongrass to use in a healing remedy passed to you by your mom, roses that remind you of your grandfather, palms that resemble those that grow in a place you visit every year, or a tree like the one in your childhood backyard.

Your garden can also be a place to create new stories with plants that support how you'll belong moving forward—honoring rituals, routines, and priorities you choose to continue or create. You may decide to make a Sunday morning habit of cutting fresh flowers from the garden to bring inside, to make a leafy summer hideaway for your kids to play and read in that they'll remember when they grow up, or to invite friends over to pick apples and make pie at the height of the season. You decide what you will do and what will be your culture, and it all can be supported by your garden.

OPPOSITE My daughter, Zeta, plants Jamaican *Hibiscus sabdariffa* (also known as roselle or sorrel) in our garden. I grew up enjoying a traditional Jamaican Christmas drink made from sorrel every holiday season. I loved learning more about the plant when I later lived in Jamaica as an adult, and am so glad that now I get to grow the plant and share it with my children.

two

Create a garden that works for you

The key to designing your garden wonderland is remembering that the goal is to create a space that works for *you*. The style should be exactly what you love; seating areas and walkways should support the way you envision living in the garden; and plants should be chosen based on what you want to look at, eat, experience, remember, and create.

I like to think of the garden design process as creating an overall container that you fill with opportunities for experiences that will be available to you on a daily basis or that can grow in, waiting for the right season—in your life, or in nature—for you to explore and discover them. Whether that means blueberry foraging with your kids, crafting with natural dyes, making medicinal tinctures for your community, or meditating with the morning birds, your garden can support you, providing a place and plants to accompany you as you grow.

Ahead are some steps to help you organize your overall space and get started with your own garden design.

OPPOSITE A simple bench, surrounded by lush greenery along a shady pathway, is a focal point in the garden and invites a moment to pause. Contrasting evergreen foliage from *Fatsia japonica* 'Spider's Web', Japanese holly fern (*Cyrtomium falcatum*), Kashmir cypress, and *Cordyline australis* 'Torbay Dazzler' make it a beautiful place to visit through the seasons.

Step 1: What annuals do you want to harvest, and where will they go?

Finding the most appropriate spots for your annual vegetables, herbs, and cutting flowers is top priority, since growing with the intention of harvesting—even a small pot of herbs—is such a powerful way to connect to the land we live with. In this step, you'll determine where to generally allot space within your overall landscape for raised beds, galvanized troughs, and large containers that will be dedicated primarily to annual edibles and cutting flowers. To successfully situate and grow these annuals, you have several key considerations.

SUN EXPOSURE

While there are endless options for ornamental plants that can thrive in a variety of situations and light exposures, many annual vegetables, herbs, and cutting flowers need a lot of sun for flavorful and abundant harvests so they are more limited in terms of where you can grow them. Early in the design process, it's essential to locate and reserve your garden's sunniest spots for annual food and flowers.

Most warm-season annual flowers and edibles do best with at least eight hours of summer sun. In California, where I live, that means an area with southwestern exposure. Morning sun in this location is a bonus but not required. Hot summer-afternoon rays that last into the early evening hours will help warm-season crops ripen their large, sweet fruits, such as big heirloom tomatoes, bell peppers, and eggplants, as well as larger blooms, such as zinnias and sunflowers.

Although it's important to start by putting the sunniest areas to productive use, the cooler, partly shaded areas of your garden, with a four- to six-hour dose of morning or midday sun, can still support other less sun-dependent edibles. So look to identify those spots next. For example, a spot that gets only morning sun will work for a raised bed planted with leafy salad and braising greens such as kale, chard, arugula, and Napa cabbage, or for veggies with smaller fruit, such as cherry

What are annuals?

Annuals are plants that live for less than one year. They grow for several months and then complete their life cycles by going to seed before dying (though you usually pull them out before this happens, unless you're saving the seed to grow in the following year). Annuals need to be planted each year. Most vegetables, including lettuce, tomatoes, and green beans, are annuals. Several herbs, such as basil and cilantro, are annuals, as are many cutting flowers such as zinnias and sunflowers.

OPPOSITE From-the-garden early spring harvest of tender pea shoots and other greens.

tomatoes, smaller hot and frying peppers, and green beans (rather than big heirloom tomatoes and bell peppers). Annual flowers that can grow in part sun, including snapdragons, violas, and nasturtiums, can also be planted here.

GROWING IN RAISED BEDS

I generally advise planting annual vegetables, culinary herbs, and cutting flowers in raised beds. These plants have different water requirements than other landscape plants and they thrive in well-worked, loamy soil (which you can purchase or make to fill your raised beds). Plus, planting higher up makes plants easier to tend to and harvest because you don't have to bend over so much. Because the attractiveness of annuals varies with the time of year, containing them this way can lend structure and design appeal in every season.

Make sure your raised bed or container is made of a food-safe material such as untreated wood, stone, clay, Corten steel, or galvanized metal. A raised bed of 8 feet long, 4 feet wide, and 2 feet tall is easy to harvest from either side, and you can easily walk around the perimeter of the bed. Although it can be tempting to increase the height of the bed to 3 feet, a tall bed can actually make it more difficult to amend and turn the soil, as is required seasonally, and taller or vining plants may be more difficult to harvest. When working in tighter spaces, we often build longer, narrower beds (10 feet long, 3 feet wide, and 2 feet tall) that can be accessed on just one side. This makes an efficient use of limited space.

The main access paths to your raised beds should be at least 3 feet wide so you have space to move around, work the soil, and get a wheelbarrow to the beds if needed. A wider path can feel more inviting and encourage more frequent interaction with your garden. If you are very short on space, your pathway width can be as little as 18 to 30 inches on the back side of each bed, which will be enough to get your body through for less regular harvests and basic cleanup.

OPPOSITE A group of 4 by 2 by 8-foot raised redwood beds with a central 4-foot-wide pathway make for easy access to annual crops. Pink-flowering spreading germander (*Teucrium*) softens the edges of nearby in-ground beds; trailing edible flowers and specialty herbs (including nasturtium, calendula, and 'Wild Magic' basil) along the edges of the raised beds are beautiful to look at while offering additional harvest.

SPACE ALLOTMENT

Your raised beds will likely require substantial space. Take some time to think about how much you really plan to grow.

My recommendation for most people who are interested in growing food and flowers more for the experience than for self-sufficiency is to plan for one or two raised beds (of the 8 by 4 by 2-foot size). This will give you room for a few favorites such as tomatoes, cucumbers, squash, broccoli, green beans, leafy greens, and flowers (see "Takeaway: What to plant in a starter veggie garden," page 96). If you train culinary herbs and strawberries over the edge of the bed and grow vertically on trellises, you can maximize productive space. You'll have variety with what you grow, but won't be overwhelmed.

If you opt for 4 raised beds, you'll have more flexible space to grow a wider range of plants, including some dedicated space for cutting flowers.

If you're more serious and aiming to grow a lot of your own food, you may want to use 6 to 12 beds, or even more if space allows. This will give you plenty of room for invaluable pantry crops and staples such as onions, celery, parsley, carrots, and garlic; successional plantings of cool-season favorites such as kale and broccoli; all the summer veggie favorites; larger and/or storage crops such as potatoes, sweet potatoes, and corn; as well as a full dedicated bed or two for cutting flowers. It can be nice to have a bit of extra space for experimenting with new varieties, fun flowers, and more unusual crops such as decorative gourds, which may not be essential but are enjoyable to grow.

FOOD IN THE FRONT OR BACK

I recommend growing most of your annual edibles in your backyard, as daily tending can feel easier to do with more privacy. Plus, backyards are generally more secure, especially with fencing that keeps out deer and critters and makes it safer for children to play or garden alongside you. It's easier to ensure food safety in the backyard, too, as the beds are less accessible to people and dogs passing by.

The case for including blooms

You can, and should, make space for some edible, cutting, and pollinator-attracting flowers in your raised beds, regardless of how little or big an area you have. Even tucking in just a few blooms along the edges of your beds will make a world of difference to how beautiful and bountiful your veggie beds will be, both because of the flowers themselves and because they attract pollinators that improve veggie productivity.

Some options include snapdragons, nasturtiums, calendulas, and violas, which are all edible and which you'll enjoy using in your drinks, salads, and desserts. Ranunculus, breadseed poppies, Iceland poppies, zinnias, cosmos, sunflowers, and amaranth are great choices for cutting.

All of the flowers mentioned above are easy to grow, and being able to cut and bring them indoors or share with your community will bring so much pleasure. You're already growing your own food—there's no reason you should be stuck going to the market to buy flowers.

In the front yard, evergreen plants that provide all-season structure are most important, because they will help hold the space visually throughout the seasons, making your front yard feel welcoming all year. You can incorporate food in front too, but for the most part, these won't be annual crops. Instead, they will be lower maintenance and good-looking evergreen edibles along with a few deciduous fruit trees (you'll find a list of favorites on the "Takeaway: Favorite front yard fruit trees," page 179).

That said, if the ideal or only sun exposure for your raised annual vegetable beds is in your front yard, that can work. Just make sure the space is beautiful for you to come home to each day by laying out your raised beds and pathways so they're an attractive feature of your front yard. This can include lining up the bed and pathway edges with major sight lines that extend from your home's architecture, and linking colors and textures in the raised beds with the surrounding landscape.

ABOVE 'Zeolights' calendula (pictured left) and 'Cupcakes Blush' cosmos (pictured right) are planted to soften the edges of raised vegetable beds.

Step 2: Where will you be, and what will you be doing?

Once you've set aside the space where you'll grow food, you can move on to designing an overall framework for where and how you will live in your outdoor space.

This is the time to dream big about all the wonderful things you hope to experience in your garden. You may envision an inviting patio where you can gather with friends or a secluded nook to sit and read. Your garden can be a safe but intriguing space for children to play or for teens to hang out. It can offer a fragrant entry that welcomes you home, a beautiful view from indoors, a walking circuit for meditation and phone calls, or anything else that's supportive or meaningful to you.

FUNCTIONS FOR FRONT YARDS AND BACKYARDS

In your front yard, it's especially important to consider functionality in terms of getting to and from the house. Ideally, the pathway leading to your front door is a solid surface, such as stone or concrete, that is walkable in all seasons. Additionally, you may need an accessible route for rolling garbage bins in and out for weekly pickup.

Another consideration is whether you will use the front yard for connecting with others. A front patio or flexible seating can support neighborhood gatherings. A strategically placed bench by the front door gives you a place to pause and enjoy a view or set down bags.

Most of our outdoor living occurs in the backyard, so there's usually more to consider there. You can start laying a framework for the space by figuring out and dedicating areas for the things you want to do, while also considering how you want to be and feel when you're outside, as outlined in this chapter.

If the existing yard space is sloped, it's important to create level landing areas to stand or sit in, which can make a huge difference in terms of how secure and safe a space feels. You'll also want to include areas of shade to support comfortable seating and gathering.

Make space for a harvest station

You may find it helpful to add a simple outdoor work station in your garden. It can include a washable work surface with an adjacent water source/ spigot or sink, where you can clean and process your vegetable and flower harvests or even arrange a bouquet of fresh flowers. To avoid wilted harvests, situate the workspace near your veggie beds, in shade, or under an umbrella.

OPPOSITE A thrifted vintage sink atop simple wooden legs adjacent to the raised annual vegetable bed area makes a useful work space for harvesting veggies and arranging flowers from the garden.

A rustic dining table made from reclaimed lumber is set directly amid dedicated cutting flower beds with a view of annual vegetables growing nearby. Nearby cherry and oak trees cast afternoon-into-evening shade.

GATHERING SPOTS

As opposed to your raised annual edible beds where you were prioritizing sun, now you want to locate shade that will be the site for your primary gathering area. If you enjoy having friends and family over for afternoon drinks and dinner, find a spot in your garden that gets afternoon-into-evening shade and reserve that for a lounging or dining area. If you're seeking a work-from-home or lunchtime gathering spot, your priority may be a spot with midday shade. Either way, try to set aside enough space to accommodate flexible group sizes.

After you've found a spot with natural shade, supplement it as needed. You may have to make or buy a structure or add an umbrella. You can also opt to plant a larger tree to provide better coverage than an umbrella and save you the cost of building a pergola or other shade structure.

For outdoor dining, situate your dining table as close as possible to the door nearest your kitchen so that it's easy to access and helps to make outdoor dining a regular part of your life. If your layout allows, consider placing your outdoor dining area among, or in view of, your annual raised beds to create an immersive experience that highlights the connection between the food you've grown and the meals you'll be eating.

OTHER SEATING AND DESTINATIONS

Aim to create one or more additional destinations in your landscape. You don't need a huge yard to do this—simply placing a comfy chair in any part of the garden will signify the purpose of the space and invite interaction.

My favorite backyard pastime is lounging in a comfortable chaise under a tree, where I can read while sipping a glass of wine, and feel immersed in nature and away from my regular busy life. I also love having a small patch of lawn where I can set down a blanket to share with my kids, walk barefoot, or lie down on.

Some people have a specific dream of kicking back in a hammock, while others imagine a pair of club chairs for morning coffee with their partner. A focal point bench or sculptural seating element at the far end of a space can anchor your view and encourage you to walk out into your garden and experience it.

PATHWAYS TO GET YOU THERE

Once you've planned out a few flexible destinations, devise clear pathways to connect them. The more simple and streamlined your patios and pathways, the more your plants will take center stage. For the most part, it's fine to use simple gravel or decomposed granite (also known as DG), as they are classic path materials and have the benefit of being water-permeable so that moisture can soak into the ground. These materials are also less expensive than flagstone or brick, which means you can invest your available budget in the plants that will add so much to your life. To contain the gravel in your path, steel pathway edging looks much better and lasts longer than plastic, without warping; it is worth the investment. I recommend that more solid hardscape—such as stone pavers, brick, or concrete—be used where your backyard garden connects to your house, such as a patio or landing outside your back door. A paved or other permanent surface in these locations is better for all-season use and will lessen the possibility of your tracking loose gravel or DG into your home.

Step 3: What do you want to see, and how do you want your garden to feel?

After you've situated your food production and yourself in your garden, consider how you want your outdoor space to look and feel. In the same way that you might consider decorating your living room to be an expression of your personal style, you can design your garden to reflect your tastes and preferences as well. There is a learning curve to selecting and growing plants, but your garden will feel so much more comfortable and supportive if it really feels like a personal expression.

CHOOSE A DESIGN DIRECTION

To get a sense of what's possible and what you like, look through photos in books, magazines, and online; walk your neighborhood for inspiration; or consider other public or private landscapes you find inspiring. You can even refer to the decor and hues inside your home to get a sense of what makes you happy, so that you can bring elements used inside your house to your outside space.

Beyond looks, how do you want to feel in your garden? Do you crave the familiarity and abundance that big blooms and recognizable harvests can inspire? Is your goal a more natural or wild energy that native and pollinator-attracting plants would support? Do you want to recreate the vibe of a warm-weather getaway with bold colors, broad foliage, and fun succulents? Knowing the feeling you hope to evoke can help you narrow in on the specific elements that will help you achieve it.

Certain plants can help to establish a specific look and feel. For example, lavender, silvery gray foliage, citrus, and roses create a Mediterranean look. Architectural foliage such as yuccas, acacias, or conifers can offer a more contemporary style. Classic blooms such as iris and hydrangeas paired with round-leaved foliage are more traditional.

Color can also dramatically impact the energy of your outdoor space. Are you dreaming of something serene and green or something vibrant and colorful? Eye candy with lots of contrast, or a plot that's muted and natural? There are no right or wrong choices, and you can choose different palettes for different parts of your garden. The idea is simply to be intentional about the appearance and feeling of the space that you are working to create.

OPPOSITE A simple gravel pathway, lined with repeated plantings of native *Heuchera maxima* and *Lomandra* Breeze, allows access to the rear part of this backyard garden.

RELATE TO WHAT'S AROUND YOU

Because good design refers to its surroundings, think about how you will connect your new garden to the style of your home and existing landscape. If, for example, your home's exterior color is a medium beige or other neutral color, using lush green leaves and strong color in the garden will help bring your property to life. If your home is painted a cool gray or darker tone, icy silver and variegated hues in the garden will really pop, as will blooms in a range of shades from jewel tones to pastels. If there's a dark-colored trim on your home's windows or other strong color element to the exterior, consider repeating that color in the landscape—with dark-painted fencing, accent walls, firepits, or garden furniture—as a way to link the overall look of your home and garden.

This doesn't mean you're obligated to mimic your home's style outdoors. If your preferred garden aesthetic is very different from the exterior style of your home, just aim to find a way to bridge them, whether it's with paint or plant colors, furniture choices, or some other element.

OPPOSITE The dark color of the painted house exterior is repeated in a dark-trimmed railing with simple, modern cabling. Contrasting foliage colors and textures from variegated shell ginger (*Alpinia zerumbet*), 'Blue Arrow' juniper, and *Euphorbia* Blackbird alongside blooms of hot pink *Salvia chiapensis* and orange *Epidendrum* pop against the dark background.

Step 4: What matters to you, and how can you make your garden meaningful?

Remember that your garden wonderland is a place for you to be and grow. I recommend incorporating personal elements into your landscape that imbue the space with deeper meaning and make it fertile ground for what really matters to you. Take time to think about how your plants and whole garden can connect you to family stories, childhood memories, cultural histories and identities, hobbies, and ritual and ceremonial practices. These may be strong existing elements in your life, or your design may be more about inspiring creativity and new directions you want to develop.

Whatever you decide to plant in your garden, you are sowing the literal seeds of what matters to you—or your dream of what matters— so that you can experience the meaning that grows from them. What follows are specific memories and requests from some of my clients over the years that might provide inspiration for your own garden. I encourage you to follow any possibilities that come to mind and see where they lead.

ABOVE Fruiting banana (pictured left) and hollyhock (pictured right) are favorite heritage plants for some of my clients.

- My grandmother always had daffodils, and I remember how delighted she was when they popped up each spring. I want to create the same experience in my garden so I can enjoy it and my kids know that feeling too.
- It's really important to me to create welcoming space that I'm able to share with my neighbors.
- I grew up blackberry foraging. I'd like to have that taste and feeling close again.
- We love to cook traditional Chinese food and often can't find the special vegetable ingredients easily.
- Growing up, I'd visit my grandparents in Ohio every summer. My grandma always had tomatoes growing near the main door. I loved brushing the tomato foliage to release its scent and now I want to grow tomatoes for their fragrant leaves almost more than the fruit.
- I want to include the special irises a friend's mom gave me and plants that mark important life events, like the birth of my kids.
- I grew up in the Midwest and love the look of hollyhocks and cornflowers. They remind me of where I'm from.
- I want to take this formal European-inspired garden and make it a Black space, with flowers in my favorite colors and foods from Black diaspora cuisines. I want to make it a place where I know, deep down, that I belong.
- I grew up in India but really found myself, came out as queer, and got free in California. I'd like to make a really Californian dream garden, but with bright orange marigolds everywhere, to celebrate this special place I love so much.
- Our favorite places in the world are Italy, where my family is from, and Hawaii, where we vacation and got married. We want to make a garden that reminds us of those places.
- My family is from Poland and I've recently been learning how to make Polish folkloric art. There is a tradition of using vegetable dyes for this, and I'd love to learn more about what to grow for natural dye and have space to experiment with that.
- Bright vibrant colors remind me of my childhood in El Salvador. That's what I like. It feels like home.
- I'd like to be able to make my own medicine for my family and kids.
- I want a canopy of feathery palm foliage to recreate the shady space and relaxation I felt playing in my childhood backyard in Singapore.
- I spent a formative time in my life on a farm in a rural area and loved it. Though we live in the city now, I want to bring that farm feeling to our garden so my son grows up with it.
- I want to see beauty every day.

three

Use plants for form, function, and delight

Becoming skilled at garden design can take time. This chapter introduces some key concepts and walks you through my planting design approach, in which trees, shrubs, and perennial flowers and edibles are added to a garden in specific layers. Even if you've never planted anything in your life, this information will give you a solid idea about how to use plants to transform your outdoor space into a garden wonderland.

Note that all the plants you'll see featured in this book are ones that thrive in our San Francisco Bay Area landscapes, where we typically have warm, dry summers and mild winters without much frost or prolonged freezing temperatures. If you see a plant that you'd like to include in your own garden, research it to see if it will thrive where you live. If not, consult staff at your local independent nursery for a good regional substitute that has similar characteristics.

OPPOSITE *Fatsia japonica* 'Spider's Web' and Japanese holly fern (*Cyrtomium falcatum*) contrast and delight.

Key design concepts

Before deciding where you'll place plants in your garden wonderland, it's helpful to understand some important ideas upon which you can build your design. Gather any notes, plant wish lists, and sketches you've been keeping up to this point, because this is where you can start filling in more details.

HARD-WORKING PLANTS

You can rely on plants to achieve a lot of your garden design goals. It's important, however, to mostly use a carefully chosen plant palette of what I consider "hard-working" plants: These plants serve multiple functions and are often evergreen perennials that are good for cutting, attracting pollinators, defining space, and/or offering flowers, fruit, or other features that highlight the season. They are not plants, such as flowering crabapples, peonies, wildflowers, or tulips, for example, that have very short bloom times and don't offer much visual impact when they are not in bloom, or that need to be replanted so often that they cannot form the framework of a garden that looks good all year.

VISUAL BALANCE

Creating a space with aesthetic appeal and that feels good to be in is very much about establishing visual balance. This means repeating and distributing elements with similar visual weight, color, and/or texture. For example, if your raised vegetable beds are on the left side of the garden, you can balance the right side of the garden with another element or elements that have a similar visual weight—perhaps a dining patio or a shade structure. If two visually heavy elements are both located at the rear of your garden, consider situating a third, similarly weighted element (perhaps a substantial firepit or fountain) farther forward and toward the center of the space to help balance the garden front to back.

OPPOSITE Hard-working plants with a mix of textures and leaf shapes are balanced across this important front yard garden view. *Pittosporum tobira* 'Wheeler's Dwarf', lamb's ears (*Stachys byzantina*), and Santa Barbara daisies (*Erigeron karvinskianus*) are low-growing pathway edgers that offer year-round interest and attract pollinators. A glossy leafed loquat tree provides handsome evergreen foliage and fruit to harvest each spring.

This goes for plants as well. Within each layer of plants and through-out your landscape, you should repeat prominent colors and textures at balanced intervals. If, for example, you've located a large, silvery fruiting olive tree in the back left part of the garden, you can balance that color and heft by adding two silvery pineapple guava shrubs at the front right, and perhaps placing a grouping of silvery lavender, astelia, or adenanthos toward the front and off-center. Or, if you choose a Japanese maple with rich plum-colored foliage, repeat its hues on the other side of the garden with burgundy loropetalum, wine-colored coral bells, or dark-toned New Zealand flax. If the wispy texture of bamboo is dominant in one part of the garden, you can repeat that texture somewhere on the other side of the garden using coleonema, feathery acacias, or wispy grasses.

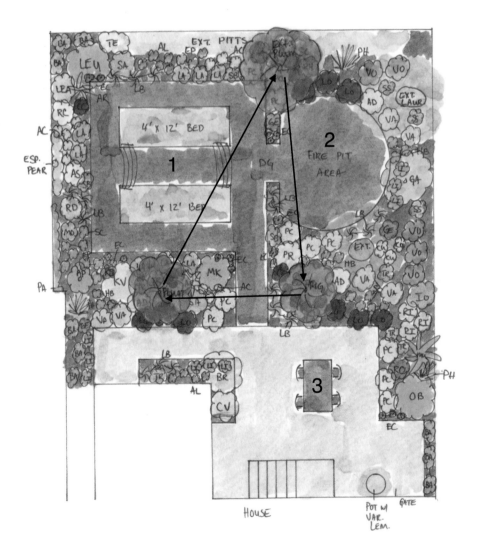

TRIANGULATION

The term *triangulation* refers to placing key elements (both plants and other features such as trellising and seating areas) in triangles rather than placing them in straight rows or on a grid, which can end up looking flat and two-dimensional. In larger landscapes, smaller vignettes, or in veggie beds, aim to place odd numbers of plants, or plant groupings, in a staggered layout so that when you step back, they form a triangle or a series of connected triangles. This will add dimension and make your garden more visually interesting and dynamic.

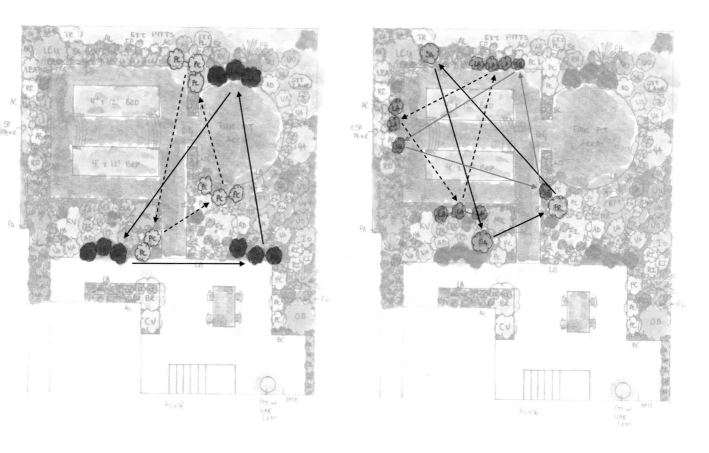

OPPOSITE Raised wooden veggie beds (1), a fire pit area (2), and dining table (3) are balanced across the landscape, as are single-trunk fruit trees, represented by arrows.

ABOVE Evergreen foliage in lime and burgundy (above left) and purple, blue, and pink flowering perennials (above right) are triangulated to add visual energy and movement to this backyard space.

FOLIAGE CONTRAST

Throughout your garden, and especially when thinking about creating special views or vignettes, situate plants with different foliage colors or textures alongside each other. In this way, the visual attributes of each plant grouping contrast and stand out. This can especially help with incorporating less-attractive perennial edibles into the landscape. Edible asparagus, for example, can look messy on its own, but its wispy foliage is beautiful when planted next to a dramatic, broad-leaved canna or dark glossy green citrus.

COLOR PALETTES

Think back to ideas that you came up with as you read through Chapter 2, in terms of how you want your garden wonderland to look and feel, then choose color palettes for both foliage and flowers. If you're just getting started, you'll likely create the most satisfying results if you keep it simple with two to four foliage colors and two to four flower hues. Because you're aiming to create a productive garden, you'll be incorporating a range of plants for floral and edible harvest that can be disparate in appearance. So, it's even more important that, where possible, you use foliage and bloom colors that link together visually and are repeated across the landscape.

Think about a foliage scheme first, starting with the colors that you know make sense for the space. Blue or chartreuse foliage can tie in with existing plantings; burgundy foliage can add saturated color to a sunny spot that may look washed out without it; silver, gold, or variegated foliage can brighten up a shady area or provide contrast against a dark backdrop.

Once you've selected one color, add a few more to round things out. Here are a few simple foliage color palettes to consider:

- **Serene:** greens, variegated (green with white), chartreuse
- **Punchy:** bright green, burgundy, orange, gold
- **Cool:** dark green, blue, silver

Once you've settled on a basic foliage color scheme, select a few flower hues that you'd like to see repeated in the space. A few simple flower color palettes I really like are:

- **Vibrant jewel tones:** fuchsia pink, vivid purple, and orange
- **Soft and warm:** peachy apricot, pale pinks, and rust with blue-purple for contrast
- **New neutral:** butter-yellow, lavender, and white, with pops of burgundy for saturation

OPPOSITE, LEFT Though all are shades of green, the varying textures of (shown clockwise from top left) *Cercis canadensis* 'Hearts of Gold', *Farfugium japonicum* var. *giganteum*, *Asparagus densiflorus* 'Myers', and *Coprosma* 'Marble Queen' contrast and allow each to shine.

OPPOSITE, RIGHT 'Inkblot' mangave and *Coprosma* 'Pina Colada' are a colorful, high-contrast combination.

Deep pink *Salvia* 'Wendy's Wish', purple *Trachelium caeruleum* 'Hamer Pandora', and orange kangaroo paw (*Anigozanthos*) blooms play off of blue *Agave franzosinii* and fruiting prickly pear (*Opuntia* 'Burbank Spineless') cactus. Assorted citrus and *Pittosporum* provide evergreen leaves.

Planting design in layers

You've dedicated raised bed space for your annual edibles and cutting flowers (see Chapter 2) and reviewed some key design concepts. Now you can decide which perennial plants you'll place in what I think of as layers throughout the rest of the garden. These include both evergreen and deciduous ornamental and edible trees, shrubs, vines, and flowers. Take the time to choose plants for each layer that will give you the most potential for experience, beauty, connection, and belonging.

When at all possible, let plants do architectural work, such as providing shelter, shade, screening, and boundaries. This creates a needed structural framework, adds sensory appeal, and builds in opportunities for production.

> ### What are perennials?
>
> Trees and perennial shrubs, flowers, and edibles can live for years. Some are evergreen and keep their leaves all year, while others are deciduous (lose their leaves), die down, or should be cut back to the ground for parts of the year before they pop back up in a future season.

LAYER 1: CREATE A BACKDROP

Use evergreens, espaliered fruit trees, or paint (yes, paint!) as a backdrop to create a sense of security, softness, and enclosure in your space. A consistently attractive backdrop will keep your garden looking good all year as the edible, medicinal, and blooming plants you may include change in appearance throughout the seasons.

Whether you garden in the front yard or backyard, you may need to address privacy and screening issues as you create a backdrop. Is your home's foundation overly exposed and in need of softening? Are there eyesores, such as a telephone pole or an adjacent roofline, that might be nice to obscure? Neighboring windows looking down over your potential patio or gathering space? Unattractive fence lines? All these issues can be remedied, and the following are your main tools.

Evergreens

Almost without exception in our garden designs, my team and I aim to create "green rooms" where our clients are surrounded by lush plants and can relax and unwind.

Bulkier, taller evergreen trees and shrubs are great for screening and building a lush perimeter. I recommend choices that are edible, that provide material for cutting flowers and foliage, and/or that feed pollinators.

Ficus nitida is an evergreen backdrop for a mixed planting that includes fruiting pineapple quince (*Cydonia oblonga*), *Salvia* 'Wendy's Wish', 'Chinotto' orange, and more.

Here are some of my go-to evergreen plant choices to create a backdrop.

EVERGREENS WITH FOLIAGE FOR CUTTING	EVERGREENS WITH FLOWERS FOR CUTTING AND POLLINATORS	EVERGREEN EDIBLES*
Acacia	Azalea, larger types	Avocado
Cedar	Camellia	Bamboo, clumping/noninvasive varieties with edible shoots
Dwarf evergreen magnolia	Cape honeysuckle (*Tecoma capensis*)	Culinary bay laurel (*Laurus nobilis*)
Elaeagnus	Giant bird of paradise (*Strelitzia nicolai*)	Citrus, non-dwarf types including orange, grapefruit, and tangerine
Fruitless olive	*Grevillea*, taller varieties	Fruiting olive
Juniper	*Leucadendron*, taller varieties	Loquat
Pine, especially *Pinus flexilis* 'Vanderwolf's Pyramid' and *Pinus strobus*	Mountain laurel (*Kalmia latifolia*)	Pineapple guava (*Feijoa sellowiana*)
Pittosporum	Rhododendron	*Note: These thrive primarily in mild winter climates, but in cold regions check specific varieties for winter hardiness as some may be hardy in your area.
Podocarpus		
Toyon (*Heteromeles arbutifolia*)		
Variegated holly (*Ilex aquifolium*)		

Espalier

Most of your backdrop will be evergreen, but if you have an interesting or pretty stretch of fence line that you'd like to highlight or feature, you can plant deciduous espalier fruit trees along it. Espaliers that are fan-shaped (a form commonly used with fig trees) can provide a great focal point; cordon-style espaliers (often used for apple or pear trees) create a tidy, classic look.

Paint

Painting a fence is a relatively inexpensive, high-impact way to create a cohesive backdrop for your garden so the beauty of the plants can shine. Using dark colors such as chocolate-brown, charcoal-gray, midnight-blue, or deepest green helps a fence to recede visually.

OPPOSITE (CLOCKWISE FROM TOP LEFT) Favorite evergreen foliage selections include culinary bay laurel (*Laurus nobilis*), *Pittosporum tenuifolium* 'Harley Botanica', Icee Blue podocarpus, and *Elaeagnus × ebbingei* 'Gilt Edge'.

A note on vines

Fruiting vines are not ideal for creating a backdrop because they are not attractive all year. Those such as grapes, passion fruit, kiwi, and caneberries (including blackberries and raspberries) can look messy or grow vigorously, may drop their leaves in winter, or may need to be cut back each January to stay productive and under control, so they are not good options for year-round perimeter screening in a prominent place, such as on a fence. Instead, they should go on freestanding arbors, pergolas where they can cast shade, or arches to create a walk-through experience.

If you don't have the space for a freestanding structure to support your fruiting vine and need to grow it along a fence, make sure the fence is in good shape and situate vines so they're not in main sight lines from your house or main gathering area.

TOP Vining grape climbing over a greenhouse entry makes for a charming experience. The reflected heat from the building helps the fruit sweeten up.

BOTTOM Kiwi twines over a Corten garden arbor.

LAYER 2: PLACE TALL PLANTS TOWARD THE CENTER

Just as many interior designers advise pulling furniture into the center of a room rather than pushing everything up against the walls, I recommend placing some taller plants in the interior of the garden rather than using them solely toward the rear or around the perimeter. This creates dimension and can also help to define garden rooms for different uses.

A garden wonderland includes food, so I encourage using one or more fruit trees in this layer. Because many fruit trees are deciduous, they're not suitable for backdrops, making this second layer their ideal spot. As a bonus, I've found that a lot less fruit is eaten by critters if fruit trees are planted away from fence lines (aka squirrel highways), which means you'll have more of your harvest to enjoy.

Take a moment to recall where your sunniest landscape spots are (you dedicated some of these for your raised beds.) Any remaining very bright spots in the interior of your garden, with long, hot afternoon light, are where you'll place the sun-hungry fruit trees that you want to grow. These are the ones that produce the largest, sweetest types of fruit, including peaches, nectarines, apricots, and navel oranges.

Beyond providing a harvest, remember that fruit trees can also serve other functions such as shading a patio in summer or framing a garden view. Before you plant a tree in the ground, be sure to walk around and look at the area from different angles, especially noting the key views and entrances that you and visitors to your garden will often encounter. Make sure you can see the trees from key sight lines, triangulating and adjusting their placement until the fruit tree layout is balanced and visually pleasing. If trees will be planted near a raised annual edible bed, place them where they won't block the afternoon sun from shining on your crops.

Where should I plant fruit trees?

The tricky thing about using fruit trees in your landscape is that many of them can grow with odd branching and a less graceful overall form than we are accustomed to seeing in classic ornamental trees. Because you want to make a beautiful garden, it's important that you consider different fruit trees' forms when situating them. Here's a quick reference to how I tend to place deciduous fruit trees through the garden according to their growth habit.

- **Classic, single-trunk fruit trees with attractive branching:** apple, pear, quince, plum, pluot, and apricot. These are perfect for situating in multiples within main views to define and balance the overall space.
- **Smaller focal point fruit trees:** weeping mulberry, 'Fuyu' persimmon, smaller figs (such as cultivars 'Panache', 'Violette de Bordeaux', and 'Black Jack'), pomegranate, and columnar apples. Situate these as freestanding focal points.
- **Espalier fruit trees:** apples, pears, figs, peaches, or pomegranates. Train these against an existing wall or fence as a focal point or informal boundary.
- **Fruit trees with awkward branching and a messier appearance:** peach, nectarine, cherry, and larger figs. These trees are best placed toward the rear or side of your garden, away from main views. If you have dedicated space for an orchard, save these trees for that area.

ABOVE 'Warren' pear (pictured left) and 'Wonderful' pomegranate (pictured right) are go-to fruit tree varieties for the home garden.

After you've decided where to place fruit trees, determine whether you want to incorporate any other tall ornamental trees or columnar shrubs in the interior of your garden. As with the deciduous fruit trees, triangulate and adjust their placement until their layout is balanced and visually pleasing.

LAYER 3: PLACE MID- AND GROUND-LEVEL EVERGREEN PLANTS

Next, you will add evergreen plants at the middle and foreground levels. These essential plants partner with the backdrop created in Layer 1 to complete the evergreen framework that will keep your garden looking good all year. This is especially important in winter, when deciduous fruit trees and some other plants have died back or gone dormant for the season. Note that these evergreen plants are not intended to take up your entire landscape. Instead, they function to frame the spaces you will leave open for non-evergreen perennial edibles and flowers (see Layer 4, page 53).

Mid-level evergreen plants are generally 3 to 6 feet tall. In most cases, you'll situate them in the interior of your garden beds in groupings that create visual rhythm across your landscape. Ground-level evergreens are generally 6 to 30 inches tall and are used along pathways and at the front of borders to define the edges and guide your eye through the space at the ground plane.

Since most gardens have mixed sun exposure, you ideally want to choose at least one plant that can thrive in *both* sun and shade, which you can repeat throughout your landscape to create some consistency and rhythm. You can also increase your food production by incorporating evergreen perennial edibles, like dwarf myrtle or citrus, in this layer.

When placing plants, be sure to check each plant's label for its size. Although some of the plants in the lists that follow can be placed in either the mid-level or ground level, situate them so that the shortest ones are in front and the tallest are in back.

Here are a few of my favorite mid-level evergreen plants. (Note that some dwarf citrus naturally grows a bit taller but can be pruned to remain under 6 feet tall.)

MID-LEVEL EVERGREENS THAT GROW IN BOTH SUN AND PART SHADE	MID-LEVEL EVERGREEN EDIBLES*
Abelia	Aloe vera
Agave, larger types	Chilean guava (*Ugni molinae*)
Azalea	Citrus, dwarf and naturally small types including calamondin, finger lime, and kumquat
Boxwood, larger types	
Chinese fringe flower (*Loropetalum*), larger types	Dwarf culinary bay laurel (*Laurus nobilis* Little Ragu)
Coleonema	Dwarf myrtle (*Myrtus communis* 'Nana')
Euonymus	Fruiting prickly pear (*Opuntia*)
Japanese holly (*Ilex crenata*)	Huckleberry
Manzanita (*Arctostaphylos*), mid-size types	Lavender, larger varieties
Mugo pine (*Pinus mugo*)	Mountain pepper (*Drimys lanceolata*)
New Zealand flax (*Phormium*)	Natal plum (*Carissa macrocarpa*), smaller cultivars such as 'Boxwood Beauty'
Osmanthus heterophyllus 'Goshiki'	
Pieris	'Sunshine Blue' blueberry
Pittosporum, compact types	Upright rosemary
Westringia	*Note: These thrive primarily in mild winter climates, but in cold regions check specific varieties for winter hardiness as some may grow in your area.

OPPOSITE *Agave franzosinii* is a favorite mid-level evergreen that can offer a classic or modern look. Here, it pairs well with purple-blooming sea lavender (*Limonium perezii*), and serves as a foreground to deciduous perennial edibles that include weeping mulberry, elderberry, and blackberries. Full-size culinary bay and other ornamentals are an evergreen background.

Here are ground-level plants I recommend because they remain full all the way to the base. They also tend to do well when planted in part shade or part sun.

GROUND-LEVEL PLANTS THAT GROW IN BOTH PART SUN AND PART SHADE

Alpine strawberry (*Fragaria vesca*)

Coral bells (*Heuchera*)

Dwarf boxwood

Dwarf Chinese fringe flower (*Loropetalum*)

Hellebore (*Helleborus*)

Liriope

Semi-evergreen flowering perennials including Santa Barbara daisies (*Erigeron karvinskianus*), lamb's ears (*Stachys byzantina*), and germanders (*Teucrium*)

Shorter conifers including *Chamaecyparis pisifera* 'Golden Mop', *Pinus strobus* (Nana Group), and *Juniperus squamata* 'Blue Star'

Shorter succulents including varieties of *Aeonium*, agaves, aloes, and echeveria

Some evergreen grasses and grasslike plants including *Lomandra*

Wintercreeper (*Euonymus fortunei*)

LAYER 4: ADD NON-EVERGREEN PERENNIAL PLANTS FOR HARVEST AND COLOR

After you've situated evergreens to create a framework (Layers 1 and 3) and trees are located to add vertical dimension (Layer 2), Layer 4 is where you will place all the other perennial flowers and edibles that will grow at the lower and middle levels of your garden. These plants are highly productive or showy in a single season—for example, they may have gorgeous spring blooms or bushels of tasty summer fruit—but don't look great all year, perhaps they lose their leaves or need to be cut back to the ground in winter. For this reason, they should be tucked between everything situated in Layers 1 to 3, so that when they're not at their peak, the evergreens will carry on the show.

Mid-level perennials for harvest

Remember that you will grow *annual* vegetables and blooms, as well as most of your smaller culinary herbs, in raised beds. In this layer, you are adding *perennial* edibles and important flowers for harvest that don't belong in your raised veggie beds. You can place plants in this layer in any open spots with the appropriate light exposure.

Here are some of my favorite mid- and low-level perennial edibles and flowers for harvest that grow well in a home garden.

MID- AND LOW-LEVEL NON-EVERGREEN PERENNIAL EDIBLES FOR SUNNIER SPOTS	MID- AND LOW-LEVEL NON-EVERGREEN PERENNIAL EDIBLES FOR SHADIER SPOTS	MID- AND LOW-LEVEL NON-EVERGREEN PERENNIAL FLOWERS FOR HARVEST
Artichoke	Chokeberry (*Aronia*)	Dahlia, larger types
Asparagus	Elderberry, green, gold, or burgundy foliage	Hydrangea
Blueberry, deciduous varieties	Fiddlehead fern, including lady fern (*Athyrium filix-femina*) and ostrich fern (*Matteuccia struthiopteris*)	Lilac
Cardamom		Peony
Cardoon		Rose
Lemongrass	Fruiting red currant (*Ribes rubrum*)	
Rhubarb	Myoga ginger (*Zingiber mioga*)	
Saffron crocus	Taro (*Colocasia esculenta*)	
Turmeric		

Repeat blooming roses (pictured left) provide a floral harvest for many months. Select multiple blueberry varieties for an extended harvest season.

Mid-level perennial flowers for color in the landscape

In this layer, you will also choose perennial blooms for impactful floral color at different times of the year. Plant mostly longer blooming deciduous or semi-evergreen perennial flowers in multiples throughout your landscape. Always triangulate and balance so that your chosen color scheme appears in a rhythmic way.

These floral superstars serve multiple functions: They carry color throughout the garden, they produce flowers for cutting, and they attract pollinators. Those with an asterisk are edible or medicinal too.

SUPERSTAR PERENNIAL FLOWERS			
*Agastache**	Gaura	Peruvian lily (*Alstroemeria*)	*Trachelium*
Arctotis	Geum	Reblooming iris	*Verbena*
Canna	Lavender (*Lavandula*)*	*Rudbeckia*	Wallflower (*Erysimum*)
Digiplexis	Ornamental grass (for seed heads)	Sage (*Salvia*)*	Yarrow (*Achillea*)*
*Echinacea**	Penstemon	*Scabiosa*	

LAYER 5: TUCK IN PLANTS FOR ADDITIONAL MEANING AND DELIGHT

At this point, you have an all-season framework that includes harvest and color. Lastly, add plants that you really love but that don't quite fit the qualifications of being hard-working, as outlined in Layers 1 to 4.

Refer back to your wish list to see if there's anything that doesn't yet have a home. In this final layer, you can find a place for these special but more single-function plants that may offer scents, seasonal experiences, habitats, or memories that you want to hold close. You are not relying on them to shape your landscape but to bring more meaning, wonder, and joy in your garden. I think of this final layer as designing to build in the thrill and awe of whatever makes the space truly wonderful for you.

OPPOSITE Mid-level perennial flowers for color: 'Cerise Queen' yarrow (pictured left) and *Verbena bonariensis* (pictured right)

ABOVE Native California poppies are a final layer of planting that celebrate the spring season, tucked in among hardworking evergreen *Senecio mandraliscae*, New England hair sedge (*Carex testacea*), and fruiting pineapple guava (*Feijoa sellowiana*).

four

Edible wonderlands

Food is the driving force behind the gardens you'll meet in this chapter. Fruit, culinary herbs, and vegetables partner with clean design, floral touches, and family histories in a series of outdoor gardens that are as delicious to look at as they are to eat. Whether you grow a little or a lot, the key is to make space for food in your garden.

OPPOSITE A summer garden harvest is inspiring in every way.

Beauty + bounty

The Sher family home sits on a hogback: a spot of land that slopes deeply on the sides, dropping into ravines that have been eroded by rainwater over time. It's the perfect perch from which to take in their nearly three acres of hillside, cloaked mainly in native plants including coast live oak (*Quercus agrifolia*), California bay (*Umbellularia californica*), toyon (*Heteromeles arbutifolia*), and buckeye (*Aesculus californica*).

The land was untamed when Pam Sher and her late husband, Merritt, bought the property in the early 1980s, and that was part of the draw. They lived alongside families of deer that passed through to the creek below, as well as hawks, jays, and quail. Over the years, they gardened on parts of the landscape that would allow it—managing poison oak, Scotch broom, ticks, and yellowjackets that had claimed the space. Bit by bit, they established a network of paths to traverse the terrain, while preserving and living in harmony with much of the wildness that first drew them to this space.

Most recently, Pam and her daughter Lacey revived a remote 35 by 75-foot plot that was designed as much for hard-working production as for its stunning beauty. "Previously this was a throwaway area," Pam says of the site, noting its prior inaccessibility and distance from the house. But as it was largely flat with a sunny exposure, this site was one of only a few expanses on the property that had any real potential for cultivation. Some years ago, they cleared and graded the area, which has had different lives—first as a family wedding site and then as a rustic, in-ground veggie patch—before its current incarnation. Now it's home to fourteen generous raised beds overflowing with vegetables, herbs, fruit, and blooms nearly all year round. "Here in Northern California, we have so much from which to pick and choose in order to create a wonderful mélange of flowers and vegetables," Pam says. "My garden is truly eclectic and satisfying with the stuff of my dreams and childhood memories."

OPPOSITE To blend into the existing landscape, the raised beds are colored with a food-safe blue-gray stain. A footed urn holds a 'Chinotto' orange tree, underplanted with *Calibrachoa* Terra Cotta and New Zealand hair sedge (*Carex testacea*). The family always grows corn, a favorite of Merritt's.

BELOW Pam's morning ritual includes taking a meditative walk down a narrow path to the vegetable garden. "When I get here, I experience this incredible stillness and beauty," she says. With her daughter Lacey, she harvests what's at its peak.

RIGHT The dining area is located in all-day shade for comfortable gathering. Eating food that's grown in adjacent beds highlights the connection the family has with the land.

OPPOSITE Lacey, a vegan chef, wanted a dedicated space to grow the family's fruits, veggies, and herbs and experiment with specialty crops. She says, "I love to watch things grow and see the life cycle from start to finish. You can see how much energy, water, and work things take to manifest."

ABOVE Lacey transforms the bounty into dishes that she shares with family and friends, and she sends everyone home with just-picked produce. "The garden is a place to create community and commune over food," she says.

A wide central pathway and generous spacing between raised beds maximizes production and access. Angular cutouts, formal urns, and whimsical overhead trellising make being in the garden feel special and reflect Pam's fondness for English and European-style gardens. Color and texture are thoughtfully repeated in the raised beds for visual interest.

OPPOSITE (CLOCKWISE FROM TOP LEFT) 'Rosa Bianca' eggplant; not-yet-ripe ají amarillo; purple shiso; birdhouse gourd (*Lagenaria siceraria*)

ABOVE Having a shaded workspace, ideally with a sink, is important so that harvested crops don't wilt in the sun and heat, and the vegetables and flowers can be comfortably cleaned, processed, and arranged.

TOP RIGHT Blooms in pale pink, buff, and burgundy were planted because Pam likes bouquets in those colors to bring inside her home.

BOTTOM RIGHT Bee boxes receive ample morning sun, which helps the bees stay healthy, and are located where their active flight path is not disrupted by main garden walkways.

takeaway

USE HERBS AND STRAWBERRIES TO CREATE BEAUTIFUL RAISED ANNUAL BEDS

Make your raised annual beds look as gorgeous as the rest of your garden.

▸ Start by placing perennial herbs and strawberries in small groups at the outer edges of the raised beds. Triangulate those groups, and check to see how they look from various important views. These perennials will look good all year, even when the annuals inside the bed fade away.

▸ Keep in mind herbs' foliage textures and colors, and place them so they contrast with each other—for example, place fine-leaved thyme next to broad-leaved strawberry or sage.

▸ For design purposes, you'll likely plant more perennial herbs than you'll use to cook and eat. Surplus herb foliage is fragrant and beautiful to cut and use in arrangements or when left to flower in the garden. Flowering perennial herbs such as sage, oregano, and thyme are a favorite food source for bees and other pollinators, so the more you plant, the more pollinators you'll attract to increase your vegetable harvest.

OPPOSITE (CLOCKWISE FROM TOP LEFT) Everbearing strawberries; tarragon against sweet potato; 'Berggarten' sage and 'Genovese' basil; Italian parsley and variegated lemon thyme

Invitation outside

Creating a view from indoors was top of mind for Karen and Peter Lin when they reimagined their backyard. Large windows from their main living area frame a retaining-walled patio and hillside lot that slopes steeply up, so they wanted to swap uninspired plantings with a living tapestry that beckoned them outdoors.

Karen also longed for an edible-filled space reminiscent of her childhood garden in Taiwan, where she often climbed her family's guava tree to sit and read. "My father was a very good gardener," she says. "We had a big yard that was initially a dump—after he cleaned it up, he grew bananas, papayas, grapes, guava, Chinese okra, and persimmons. Our garden became known throughout the neighborhood."

With a new mix of lush foliage, flowers, and edibles, the couple's backyard has become one of their favorite destinations, with much to harvest year round, including bananas, blueberries, kumquat, persimmons, lemons, grape, pomegranate, and olives that they brine—not to mention an entire menu's worth of herbs and vegetables, including many varieties of Asian greens that they've spent several years growing from seed to narrow down their favorites. "I'm just happy to see food grow, and I think my father would be happy," Karen says. "The banana tree is for him."

When she's not tending her roses, veggies, or the many plants given to her by friends, Karen relaxes and reads on a built-in bench. Peter enjoys an evening cocktail or a glass of wine while grilling or sitting and listening to the water feature. Their friends and family—who come for meals, Quaker meetings, parties, and taiji (tai chi)—love their landscape, too, and visitors often stand on the deck and simply take in the view. "It's been so enriching to our lives to be with nature, and we enjoy being out here and entertaining much more," Peter says. "The garden really adds a whole different dimension to our house and the way we live."

OPPOSITE The lower part of the hillside is easier to access, so it was planted with perennial edibles and cutting flowers. The orange, yellow, red, and silver color scheme includes New Zealand hair sedge (*Carex testacea*), *Leucadendron*, citrus, olives, artichoke, agaves, and California poppies. 'Fuyu' persimmon is a focal point deciduous fruit tree. Evergreens help the space to look good year round.

BELOW Karen regularly harvests specialty pea shoots and other crops for meals.

RIGHT Raised annual edible beds are terraced against the hillside. Herbs and flowers are triangulated at the edges of the beds in colors that visually connect them to the rest of the garden. Rosemary, pomegranate, and Chilean guava (*Ugni molinae*) planted on the hillside provide additional harvest.

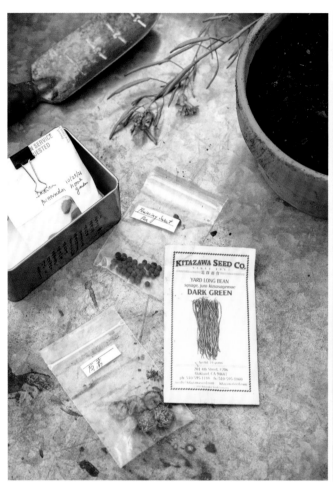

ABOVE Karen experiments with different crops, including salad mixes, braising greens, and flowers for cutting, at her work table. She orders less commonly available seeds for specialty Asian greens online and also swaps seeds with friends.

OPPOSITE (CLOCKWISE FROM TOP LEFT) Purple mizuna, komatsuna, chrysanthemum, and Chinese stem lettuce are favorite edible greens that Karen and Peter grow in the cool season.

OPPOSITE Having an inviting space to lounge draws Karen and Peter outdoors. A fruiting banana takes advantage of water that collects at the bottom of the slope. Meyer lemons are easily within reach for regular harvest.

RIGHT A friend gave Karen this queen of the night blooming cactus (*Epiphyllum oxypetalum*), which reminds her of one her dad grew when she was a child.

BOTTOM LEFT Peter and Karen learned how to brine the olives they harvested from their hillside tree.

BOTTOM RIGHT Karen loves making bouquets from cut flowers including roses, ranunculus, snapdragons, and annual greens that have gone to flower.

takeaway

HOW TO MAKE A USEFUL HILLSIDE PLANTING

Plots that slope steeply upward can be productive. Just keep a couple of guidelines in mind.

▸ In the lowest part that's most easily accessible, grow perennial edibles and cutting flowers and foliage. These productive plantings will benefit from water that drains down from higher up the hill. If the slope is super steep, create small berms around fruit trees to help them hold water around their roots and get established.

▸ Higher up, grow plants that need minimal care since they are harder to access. These can include native and pollinator-friendly plants that support wildlife and increase the productivity and health of everything else growing in your garden.

OPPOSITE Chilean guava (*Ugni molinae*) (bottom left), red-tipped *Leucadendron* (top right), and silvery fruiting olive (background) are perennial plants that provide an evergreen backdrop and seasonal fruit and cutting foliage.

A farm of their own

Charlotte Soja's family always had an edible plot, and one of her first jobs as a teenager was arranging flowers for a neighbor. She envisioned one day having space for a food- and flower-filled garden of her own. So when her parents downsized and she and her husband, Jon, bought her childhood home, their first priority was not renovating the house itself but making the landscape personal to them.

A driving force behind their garden's edible-focused design was to teach their sons, Ben and Owen, about what plants are in season at different times of year and the labor and resources required to grow them organically and sustainably. "We want the kids to appreciate good-quality food grown without chemicals and pesticides," Charlotte says. "Even when the kids are older, this will be at their core and they will come back to it."

In a deep side yard, the family's mini-farm is packed with berries, vegetables, herbs, and flowers, while artichokes, citrus, fruiting cactus, and other fruit trees are interspersed among ornamental plants in the rest of the backyard. Charlotte's vision of crafting meals from what's growing in the garden has come to life, and Ben and Owen are the harvest team who love sharing the space with friends. Jon handles much of the garden's care, mowing the lawn, weeding, and fertilizing throughout the year. "There are so many different things going on," Jon says. "Seeing things grow and change makes you pay attention and be thankful for what you have."

OPPOSITE Densely packed raised beds overflow with seasonal veggies, herbs, strawberries, and cutting flowers that draw pollinators to increase the crops' productivity. Pink and orange flowers and purple foliage are repeated to guide the eye through the space.

ABOVE Ben and Owen help Charlotte manage the harvest. Charlotte spends time each week seeking out recipes that celebrate the garden's offerings. She loves to experiment and rarely makes the same thing twice. "It's the dream to grow and learn," she says.

RIGHT Jon turns the compost, which is made from yard clippings. It goes back into planting beds to nourish the soil.

CLOCKWISE FROM TOP LEFT Bay leaves flavor bundt cake; lemon verbena and shiso add color and flavor to drinks; and pansies and cornflower are pressed and baked into shortbread.

BELOW Edible Chilean guava (*Ugni molinae*) and *Acacia cognata* Cousin Itt have fine leaves that contrast against flat edible *Opuntia* paddles.

RIGHT Charlotte and Jon made a bold design choice to paint their ranch house and retaining walls charcoal-gray, which creates a perfect backdrop to showcase a palette of high-contrast plants, including spiky *Furcraea macdougalii* in the highest bed, *Aloe tongaensis* 'Medusa' along the stairway, and groupings of silvery blue fruiting prickly pear (*Opuntia* 'Burbank Spineless').

LEFT Evergreen *Ficus nitida* provides a year round backdrop, while evergreen *Pittosporum tobira* 'Wheeler's Dwarf', *Agave franzosinii*, and *Euphorbia* 'Tasmanian Tiger' contain the front of the border. Along with other perennials, bronze-leafed canna and fruiting pineapple quince (*Cydonia oblonga*) offer color and harvest in parts of the year.

BELOW Frosty white dudleya leaves resemble a giant flower and pop against feathery green *Acacia cognata* Cousin Itt.

takeaway

ADD EDIBLE FLOWERS THAT LOOK GOOD IN YOUR VEGGIE BEDS AND ON YOUR PLATE

Planting edible flowers in veggie beds not only makes the beds prettier, it also provides more for you to harvest. Flower petals are a fun seasonal touch to add to foods, such as cooked and baked items, salads, desserts, and drinks. Choose colors for your edible flowers that tie into the hues you're using for your annual raised beds. Here are some favorite options to include.

- *Agastache*
- Alyssum
- Borage
- Calendula
- Cornflower (pictured above)
- Flowering basil, such as African blue and 'Wild Magic'
- Marigold
- Nasturtium
- Pansy
- Pinks (*Dianthus*)
- Scented geranium (*Pelargonium*)
- Snapdragon
- Sunflower
- Viola

OPPOSITE A cozy fireside sitting area—a favorite spot where the kids roast marshmallows—offers views of the surrounding landscape. Lime-green *Asparagus densiflorus* 'Myers' and *Salvia chiapensis* soften the transition to the main patio.

Homegrown retreat

Bordering open space with views of ancient oaks and the San Francisco Bay, Judy Johnson and Harold Wooten's backyard feels worlds away from the busyness of the Bay Area. Here, hawks, scrub-jays, deer, raccoons, and squirrels are among the locals that regularly visit. So, when the couple revamped their front and back gardens, they sought to refresh the spaces while maintaining the bucolic peacefulness that permeates the property.

As avid cooks, the couple prioritized having easy-to-access edibles. A lifelong gardener, Harold grew up raising flowers, vegetables, and fruit alongside his dad in Detroit, and he's now passing on these skills to his granddaughter. "My father said it would be good therapy when I got older because it keeps you close to nature," he says. "I feel closer to my father when I'm gardening and hope my granddaughter will have the same experience."

They also wanted to create spaces that invited relaxation. Judy, a retired prosecutor, executive director of the California State Bar, and superior court judge, says that the stimulation of her former workplace could be overwhelming, and the stillness of their garden offers the perfect antidote. "The garden provides respite," she says. "I can have a glass of wine and decompress without noise—all I hear are insects and the flowers moving. I really like the quiet."

This garden retreat has been deeply restorative for Harold as well. "I feel at home here. I sit and contemplate whatever comes to mind," he says. "I could spend my entire day out here, and I don't think it's time wasted. I think having a nice garden is part of the essence of life. It makes me feel part of existence. I want for nothing."

New Zealand flax (*Phormium*) and semi-dwarf mandarin citrus are part of an evergreen framework, while roses and Digiplexis provide seasonal color and flowers for cutting.

ABOVE Judy and Harold make an orzo salad with mint, basil, and tomatoes from the garden. Judy's favorite crops to grow are herbs. "We don't use a lot of salt, so we use herbs to enhance flavor," she says.

LEFT With a lawn surrounded by a shrub-and-flower border, the backyard's design is traditional—as Harold and Judy wanted it—but the border plantings are less conventional. Two favorite roses, gifts from a former colleague of Judy's, pair with agave; and perennial edibles including blueberries, assorted citrus, and Chilean guava (*Ugni molinae*) punctuate other evergreens.

OPPOSITE (CLOCKWISE FROM TOP LEFT) Harold preserves some of the harvest by canning, and he makes a family recipe for Southern chow chow—a pickled relish—using both sweet and spicy peppers from the garden; bell pepper; a waist-high raised bed makes for more comfortable harvesting; 'Spicy Globe' basil.

Harry the dog patrols the front perimeter that includes Mountain cabbage tree (*Cussonia paniculata*), giant bird of paradise (*Strelitzia nicolai*), *Acer palmatum* 'Butterfly', *Aspidistra elatior* 'Milky Way', *Blechnum* 'Silver Lady', *Coprosma* 'Pina Colada', and *Yucca recurvifolia*.

ABOVE The fenced front yard is a welcoming refuge designed mainly with evergreen foliage in harmonious textures and varying hues of green and silver. This is a favorite spot for Judy to sip her morning coffee and read. "It's not just tending to the garden," Judy says. "It's about peace of mind: having a place to sit, look at, absorb, and feel. We have a cocoon here."

RIGHT A giant rosette of *Agave attenuata* 'Kara's Stripes' is a year-round focal point that complements the heart-shaped leaves of *Cercis canadensis* 'Ruby Falls' and deep green foliage of *Pittosporum tobira* 'Wheeler's Dwarf'.

takeaway

START A SUMMER VEGGIE GARDEN

Friends who are new to gardening always ask me what they should grow, so I've put together a list to help any beginner get started. This quantity of vegetables, herbs, and flowers will fit in two standard (4 by-8 foot) raised vegetable beds. If you have room to make your beds a bit longer (perhaps 4 by 10 feet), you'll appreciate the extra growing space. If you are planting in one raised bed or the equivalent area, focus on your favorites and choose about half from the list.

Follow these general steps to get growing:

- Fill beds or containers with fresh soil, ideally an organic blend that's made for growing veggies. Top it off with 1 to 2 inches of organic compost and mix in a generous dusting of organic veggie fertilizer. Replenish the nutrients each planting season (spring and fall) by tilling in a few inches of compost and adding organic fertilizer.
- Include sturdy, beautiful, food-safe trellises for vining edibles or flowers. This is an important part of adding vertical dimension. I love to use metal trellising with a bit of patina, but wood or bamboo trellises work well too. Remember that your edible trellising is a semi-permanent element of your garden that you'll see every day and that will greatly affect the appearance of the overall space.
- Set up drip irrigation on a timer. You'll need to water frequently enough so that the soil stays moist but not soggy (like a wrung-out sponge). You can adjust the watering schedule as the weather and seasons change.
- Once your veggies start ripening, harvest them regularly—at least every two or three days—to pick veggies at their peak and to keep plants producing.

I tend to plant more densely than some sources recommend. This approach results in full, lush beds that are beautiful to look at, that enable you to grow a lot more food in a smaller space, and that experience less water loss from evaporation and competition from weeds. You'll need to prune and harvest your plants a bit more often to prevent overcrowding, but because the results are so beautiful and productive, it will be a joy to do so.

VEGGIE GARDEN SUPPLIES LIST AND HOW-TO (FOR 2 RAISED BEDS)

- **TRELLISING:** 2 to 4 large obelisks or cone style trellises
- **PERENNIAL CULINARY HERBS AND STRAWBERRIES** (to trail over the edge of the bed): 1 each English thyme, French thyme, Greek oregano, sage, tarragon; 8 strawberry plants
- **ANNUAL HERBS:** 2 to 3 each flat-leaf parsley, cilantro, Genovese basil
- **PANTRY ITEMS:** 1 celery or spring onions
- **FLOWERS** (edible, pollinator-attracting, or cutting): 1 to 2 each zinnias, cosmos, Gem marigolds; 3 trailing nasturtiums to grow over the edge; 1 calendula
- **TOMATOES:** 1 early cherry variety such as 'Sun Gold'; 1 early- to mid-season like 'Early Girl' or later season heirloom like 'Pink Berkeley Tie Dye'
- **CUCUMBER:** 1 Armenian, Persian, Suyo Long, pickling, 'Lemon', or other variety
- **GREEN BEANS:** 1 six-pack of a vining variety, such as Romano or 'Blue Lake', to grow up a trellis or 1 six-pack of any bush bean variety
- **PEPPERS OR EGGPLANTS:** 3 peppers, such as shishito or 'Jimmy Nardello'; or 3 eggplants, such as 'Fairy Tale' or 'Nadia'
- **SUMMER SQUASH:** 1 'Magda' or other bush/patio-size summer squash variety
- **MELON** (to train over the edge of the bed and along the ground): 1 cantaloupe or other favorite smaller variety; or 1 winter squash, such as delicata, butternut, or other variety
- **PURPLE BASIL:** 2 purple 'Wild Magic' and 1 African blue basil, to make your garden and food pretty
- **BRAISING GREENS:** 3 kale or Swiss chard varieties of your choice
- **SALAD GREENS**, tucked into a shadier spot in the beds: 1 six-pack arugula or other favorite salad green

Place perennial culinary herbs and strawberries around the edges of the beds, focusing on creating pretty vignettes in key views and aiming for foliage contrast. Then add flowers and purple basils, again balancing and triangulating your seasonal color for visual depth and energy. Finally, situate annual vegetables and herbs, making sure big tomatoes, eggplants, and peppers are in the parts of the beds that receive the most hours of sun each day.

Your perennial herbs and strawberries will stay in place through the seasons, softening the look of the bed and serving as consistent evergreen visual anchors. For all seasons, you can also keep one or two food-safe pots or grow bags adjacent to your veggie beds (and hooked up to the same irrigation line) to grow annual crops such as potatoes and culinary herbs such as mint that will spread widely if planted in your main veggie beds.

For a cool season garden, reduce the vertical trellising in your beds by about half and remove the tomatoes, cucumbers, green beans, peppers, eggplants, squash, basil, and melon. With perennial herbs, strawberries, and trellising in place, swap in the plants you want to grow as fall–winter crops: edible snap peas, broccoli, cabbage, braising greens (kale, chard, collards, Napa cabbage), salad greens (lettuces, radicchios), root crops (carrots, beets, turnips), and alliums (garlic, onions, shallots). Substitute violas for purple basils and add snapdragons, Iceland poppies, and calendula for winter floral color.

Over time, you'll narrow down varieties and quantities of favorite annual crops. Keep pantry crops (celery, spring onions, shallots) in your winter and summer beds. These plants have a long harvest window and can stay in your beds for months, until you're ready to cook them.

five

Floral wonderlands

Flowers are a source of joy and wonder, whether you are encountering a rare, fragrant bloom or familiar petals at your local grocery store. Embracing the sheer delight of flowers—whether for simple viewing, cutting and arranging, using for craft projects, and more—is at the center of the gardens ahead. Grow flowers, grow your joy.

OPPOSITE *Papaver somniferum* 'Lauren's Grape'

Growing home

"If you want to know the real me, you have to meet me in my garden," says Hala Kurdi Cozadd. And it's easy to understand why: her plot is a living scrapbook of her life, filled with flowers and other plants that reflect the people and places that mean the most to her.

The daughter of diplomats, Hala was born in Jordan, and during her younger years, her family moved to Germany, Saudi Arabia, Washington, D.C., and California's Bay Area, where she now lives with her husband, Bruce, and their blended family. As a child, Hala was given basil seeds, which she planted. When the plants flourished, her identity as a gardener took root. As she and her family moved, she started a new garden in each new location, and plants were her constant companions. "When you move a lot, there's a lot of loss—I envied people who grew up in one place," Hala says. "My plants are my home. Other than my family, they were the only stable thing in my life."

Today, her landscape includes fragrant citrus trees and herbs that remind her of Jordan; blossom-covered cherry trees and tulips that recall Washington, D.C.; clivias like those that bloomed on her high school grounds; *Osmanthus fragrans* that scented her college campus; fuchsias and begonias like her grandma grew; and birch, bay, and viburnum like those from previous homes in adulthood.

"I need to have flowers," Hala says, and an abundance of blooms fills her landscape in every season. "Flowers awaken all my senses. I'm constantly in awe of their color combinations. Then there are those that seduce you with their scent." Others, she adds, are very tactile, make particular sounds, and have edible appeal. Plants including fuchsia, which her mom taught her to squeeze to make a popping noise, and honeysuckle, whose nectar she and her childhood friends devoured—bring back happy memories of her younger years.

"Gardening has been one of my greatest blessings, without a doubt," says Hala. She spends part of every day in her landscape as a way to reconnect with the best parts of herself. Although she mindfully tends every inch, she says, "I don't own this garden. I'm the guardian of it. The garden is constantly giving to me, and I have to remind myself to receive. For me, it's about love and magic and healing."

OPPOSITE The outdoor dining table is placed centrally and surrounded by cut flower beds.

ABOVE When Hala started growing in this garden, she says, "I walked around and got to know the land, and had it get to know me. I walked with intention— the garden is a living, breathing thing. Before planting anything, I bless it and say a prayer. I've always done that."

RIGHT Hala keeps a journal about her garden throughout the seasons. She stores and organizes seeds in labeled plastic cases to keep them fresh.

OPPOSITE (CLOCKWISE FROM TOP LEFT) Roses, echinaceas, dahlias, and feverfew (*Tanacetum parthenium*) are all favorites for cutting.

BELOW A summer harvest of squash and eggplant.

RIGHT Hala's vegetable and cutting flower garden space features 8 raised beds, decomposed granite pathways, and a central gathering area.

TOP LEFT Grapes and their edible leaves show up often in family meals. They're planted near edible scented geraniums (*Pelargonium*) for foliage contrast.

TOP RIGHT Large, deeply lobed squash foliage contrasts with tiny Gem marigolds, an edible flower.

LEFT Hala has Russian roots on her mom's side and Italian and Turkish/Kurdish heritage on her dad's. She loves growing and cooking with plants that reflect her heritage such as Za'atar, a type of oregano used as the base of a spice mixture of the same name.

OPPOSITE Edible and pollinator-attracting flowers, such as pale-pink cosmos and purple-foliaged 'Wild Magic' basil, dress up raised bed edges. Heirloom tomatoes grow on sturdy metal tomato cages.

ABOVE Hala (with her husband, Bruce, her daughter, Nicole, and her son, Julian) says, "I feel good to have created a space that heals people. The food production literally nourishes our family, friends, and neighbors, and I want to share this space because I know what it can do for them. It's an extension of my heart and soul."

RIGHT Nicole makes bouquets from seasonal blooms, including dahlia, *Scabiosa*, dara (*Daucus carota*), *Veronica*, and basil.

takeaway

HOW TO DESIGN A GORGEOUS CUTTING FLOWER BED

If you want an abundance of varied blooms for bouquets, it's best to grow them in a dedicated spot. This could be a raised bed alongside your vegetables and herbs or a special area within your in-ground landscape. Since a cutting flower bed is intended for productive use, it can end up looking haphazard, but with a little planning, you can ensure that it looks good most of the year. Here's how.

1. Create an all-season framework for the bed. Use evergreen plants as a partial or complete bed edger or border. Great choices for in-ground beds include dwarf boxwoods, germanders (*Teucrium*), hellebores (*Helleborus*), and coral bells (*Heuchera*). Great edgers for raised beds are dusty miller (*Senecio cineraria*), pinks (*Dianthus*), strawberries, scented geraniums (*Pelargonium*), and low-growing pincushion flowers (*Scabiosa*). (Mid-level evergreens or trellising can be placed within the bed for vertical punctuation.)

2. Choose a color scheme. A good guideline is to choose one or two main flower hues to repeat in the bed, then choose another two or three colors to complement those. Think about your favorite shades to bring indoors, which may be different from what's in your landscape. Include at least one flower or foliage color that connects the bed with the rest of your outdoor space.

3. Consider flower shapes. Include three or more contrasting flower forms for beautiful beds and future flower arrangements. A good way to start is to choose a mix of spire, daisy- or open-faced, and umbel-shaped blooms, which are especially distinctive forms. Then add other flower shapes if you like.

4. With your preferred colors and flower shapes in mind, choose and place blooms. Include primarily perennials, but leave open pockets for seasonal annuals. The perennial flowers you'll use here are ones you love, but are not hard-working enough to include a lot of in your larger landscape, such as delphiniums, foxgloves (*Digitalis*), globe amaranth (*Gomphrena*), and dahlias. Group the taller plants and triangulate any others you have multiples of.

5. Fill the open pockets with annual cutting blooms, such as zinnias, *Agrostemma*, and snapdragons. Replace with other annual cutting flowers as needed each season.

continued

Here are some cutting flower possibilities by shape:

SPIRE
- *Agastache*
- Digiplexis
- Foxglove (*Digitalis*)
- Larkspur (*Delphinium*)
- Penstemon
- Snapdragon

DAISY OR OPEN-FACE
- *Agrostemma*
- *Anemone*
- Chocolate cosmos (*Cosmos atrosanguineus*)
- Chrysanthemum
- *Echinacea*
- *Rudbeckia*
- Sunflower
- Zinnia

PIN-CUSHION
- *Astrantia*
- Knautia (*Knautia macedonica*)
- *Leucospermum*
- *Scabiosa*

UMBEL
- Dara (*Daucus carota*)
- *Trachelium*
- White lace flower (*Orlaya grandiflora*)
- Yarrow (*Achillea*)

SPHERE
- *Craspedia*
- *Gomphrena*
- Ornamental alliums
- *Silene asterias*

CENTERPIECE
- Dahlia
- Iris
- *Lisianthus*
- Peony
- Peruvian lily (*Alstroemeria*)

QUIRKY
- Amaranth
- *Cerinthe*
- Columbine
- Fritillaria
- Hellebore (*Helleborus*)
- *Nicotiana*
- Sea holly (*Eryngium*)
- Tulip

OPPOSITE Evergreen dwarf boxwood fronts an in-ground planting of columbine, foxglove, *Nicotiana*, snapdragons, and *Agrostemma*.

Time to bloom

The deep backyard was a selling point when Chris Knowlton and Steve Akeson bought their home, because they wanted as much space as possible for their own urban farm. In their first few decades there, they grew bushels of produce, kept bees, raised chickens, and continually created compost in their backyard plot. But as Chris and Steve neared retirement, they longed for less work and more play, so the couple transformed the landscape from one focused on hard-working production to a garden designed for a balance of edibles, flowers, and year-round beauty.

Beds full of bright blooms used for cutting, attracting pollinators, and textile projects are highlights. The garden is filled with meaningful plants throughout: irises from a high school friend's grandmother, espaliered pears that Chris's dad had given the couple as a wedding gift, a Malaysian lime that Steve's parents brought back from their travels, and Peruvian lilies from the garden of a friend who had passed on.

Their yard is still packed with a bounty of edibles that the couple loves to share. "Anytime someone comes to our house, they go away with a bag of food," Chris says. In return, friends and neighbors gift them treats including home-brewed beer and Lao dishes made by local women who harvest their edible bamboo.

As the garden evolves, Chris and Steve have too, finding new pastimes. "We've become more focused on how to preserve—either dry, can, or pickle—the tremendous amount of food that comes out of the backyard," Steve says. Chris cuts flowers to use in arrangements and makes plant-based fabric dyes. "I felt like when I had this garden, I could do more, and then I wanted to do more," Chris says. "When I retired, I was never bored or searching for something to do because it was all there."

OPPOSITE Chris's personal getaway is at the back of the property under the shade of a fig tree. "I wanted a place I could go that was relatively hidden, where I could view the garden and be by myself," she says. "From that spot, I see the garden in a different way. I put my drink on the Adirondack chair arm, and sit there and read or knit or do nothing."

ABOVE Silvery pineapple guava (*Feijoa sellowiana*), a neighbor's orange tree above rosemary, a fig tree, pale-pink Peruvian lily (*Alstroemeria*), purple *Verbena bonariensis*, broad-leafed summer squash, 'Zeolights' calendula, and violet-colored wallflowers (*Erysimum*)

LEFT A raised annual edible bed includes corn, tomatoes, squash, and zinnias.

OPPOSITE (CLOCKWISE FROM TOP LEFT) Chris uses flowers such as echinacea to make natural dye, blooming artichoke to support pollinators, dahlias, and frilly red 'Naughty Nineties' poppies for cutting. She loves harvesting flowers, and says, "The garden grounds me in my true self and has enhanced my equanimity and calmness."

BELOW Chris and Steve are active and adventurous cooks, cocktail makers, and flower arrangers who enjoy finding new ways to use the abundance of produce and blooms.

LEFT Hugged by flowers and edibles, the central patio is an inviting room for relaxing and gathering.

A longtime fiber artist, Chris uses plants from her garden for various projects including this flower-dyed tablecloth, a memento of the blooms she grew and harvested one year. She grows plants such as indigo (*Indigofera*), cosmos, yarrow, and marigolds to make natural dyes.

takeaway

TIE YOUR GARDEN TOGETHER WITH COLOR

In designing your garden, you, like most people, probably aren't starting with a blank slate. You may have inherited a random mix of plants surrounding your house, or you may want to keep or add some favorites that don't necessarily coordinate. Here's how to use floral and foliage color to create a unified overall look.

- ‣ Choose a limited palette, such as purple and yellow.
- ‣ Repeat your chosen colors (in flowers, foliage, or both) in both in-ground and raised beds among existing plants, with regularity so the colors make an impact. Use enough to guide the eye through the space and create cohesion among wide-ranging existing plants.

Modern cottage

When Sarah Nguyen and Andrew Poon relandscaped their front yard, Sarah was sure of one thing: she wanted a garden overflowing with flowers. An admirer of English cottage garden style, she loved the idea of being able to see lush blooms in every direction. The couple also wanted the space to be low maintenance and to require minimal irrigation, since water conservation is the rule rather than the exception in their region's naturally summer-dry climate.

An unexpected plant combination was key to creating a visual tapestry in a new garden that delights and inspires joy every day of the year. The design is a play between modern and romantic: clean lines create structure, while loosely layered plantings give a billowy look. Evergreen trees and shrubs form the backbone of the garden, while floral flourishes mark the time of year: wallflower (*Erysimum*), iris, and dogwood in the spring; lavender, sea lavender (*Limonium perezii*), rose, crape myrtle, and butterfly bush (*Buddleja*) in the summer; grass plumes in the fall; and vibrant tangerines and a fragrant yuzu citrus tree (*Citrus junos*) in the winter. Bloomers including Santa Barbara daisies (*Erigeron karvinskianus*), kangaroo paws (*Anigozanthos*), and rosettes of *Agave parryi* hold space in between, with flowers or flowerlike forms that span multiple seasons. Andrew says that the changing show helps root him to the space. When different plants are at their peak, he says, "I feel connected to nature and more in tune with the seasons."

The couple's sons, Hunter and Darius, use the whole space, whether they're running or riding on the paths, exploring under plants, or helping with the harvest. While most of the homes in the neighborhood have lawns in front, Sarah and Andrew opted to go lawn-free but still have a visually restful expanse in their circular entry court. Curved benches hug the wide front path, inviting neighborliness and offering a welcoming spot for casual visits. "It's perfect—like out of a fairytale," Sarah says.

OPPOSITE Sarah has happy childhood memories of being in the garden with her mom and wanted to recreate that for their sons. The curving front path is hugged by *Pittosporum tobira* 'Wheeler's Dwarf', Santa Barbara daisies, and lamb's ears (*Stachys byzantina*).

Because the family entertains often, they wanted a welcoming entry. A generous front courtyard paved with warm-toned flagstone, interplanted with creeping thyme, invites visitors in.

ABOVE, LEFT Sarah loves being greeted by this path every time she pulls into her driveway. It's bordered by *Aeonium canariense*, *Euphorbia* 'Tasmanian Tiger', *Arthropodium cirratum*, and nandina, all water-wise evergreens with contrasting foliage.

ABOVE, RIGHT Sarah brushes 'Provence' lavender, releasing its scent.

ABOVE A soft color palette combines silver (*Teucrium fruticans*), greens (evergreen dogwood and *Calamagrostis* 'Karl Foerster'), and orange (loquat and *Coprosma* 'Rainbow Surprise').

LEFT Blooming dogwood provides spring color.

OPPOSITE A mini-orchard alongside the driveway with 'Warren' pear, Asian pear, and dwarf avocado trees incorporates evergreens for year-round good looks. Plantings include lamb's ears (*Stachys byzantina*), 'Swane's Golden' cypress, 'Big Red' kangaroo paws, and Icee Blue podocarpus.

ABOVE In the front orchard, the kids help harvest flowers including 'The Third Harmonic' alstroemeria (pictured right). Andrew, an avid cook and cocktail enthusiast, loves having access to fresh seasonal produce including avocados (pictured left). "If you want premium ingredients, growing your own is really worth it," he says.

takeaway

GET LOTS OF FLOWERS WITH LESS WORK

Because flowers are showy, colorful, and impactful, people often assume they require a lot of care. But creating a beautiful, blooming display doesn't have to be difficult. The key is choosing perennials that flower for a long stretch of time without requiring heavy maintenance.

The following are some of my favorite lower maintenance bloomers that deliver a lot of bang for the buck. Most of these plants benefit from some deadheading during their bloom season and a hard pruning each winter.

- *Aeonium* (while these do produce seasonal flowers, I grow them primarily for their rosette shape that gives an all-season floral feel)
- Digiplexis
- Gaura
- Geum
- Kangaroo paw (*Anigozanthus*)
- *Limonium*
- Penstemon
- Peruvian lily (*Alstroemeria*)
- Reblooming iris (reblooming types are often labeled as such)
- *Salvia* Wish series
- Santa Barbara daisy (*Erigeron karvinskianus*)
- Wallflower (*Erysimum*)
- Yarrow (*Achillea*)

six

Healing wonderlands

Healing happens in many ways, including in our gardens. The landscapes in this chapter show how designing an intentionally peaceful environment, growing food and medicinal herbs, taking part in plant-based spiritual practices, and honoring beauty can be a tonic for our bodies, minds, and spirits. Make your garden a space where healing can happen.

OPPOSITE Medicinal elderberry (*Sambucus nigra* ssp. *cerulea*)

Healing haven

A tapestry of colorful and fragrant flowers, chirping birds, and mouth-watering edibles greets you the moment you step into Elizabeth Horn and Zach Nelson's cottage garden. Deliberately designed to feed all the senses, the space restores everyone who enters. "It's my sanctuary. I visit the garden every morning and evening—it starts and ends my day with something beautiful," Elizabeth says.

What was once an unused tennis court is now a lush landscape, created for the couple's daughter, Sophia, who has autism. Her homeschool teachers use it as a living nature lab—watching bees collect nectar, crushing lavender to release its scent, and picking cherry tomatoes—to teach Sophia about the cyclical nature of food production. Elizabeth has spent more than two decades developing networks of experts to help us better understand autism spectrum disorder (ASD) and she often hosts meetings of researchers, clinicians, educators, and families affected by autism in her cottage garden. "I have had many requests for photos and planting plans from these visitors," she explains. "It's an inspiration to all who walk through it, as well as a clinically proven way to lower the anxiety that so often accompanies living with autism."

Of the efforts she leads at her 2m Foundation, she says, "I spend most of my time in my head working on things that most people still believe are impossible. But I had the plan for this wonderful garden in my head—and look, it's even better than I imagined. It gives me hope that all the work we do every day for people dealing with the challenging impact of ASD will eventually bear fruit as well. We just need to stay true to the vision and keep sharing it with others.

"When you're doing difficult things, having a strong spiritual ecosystem around you is a prerequisite. You must have supportive people, supportive spaces that shelter you. I talk to my garden, really love every minute I spend wandering through. You have to put that love into the molecules of a space. People walk in and that's what they feel."

Just as the family has revitalized the garden, the garden revitalizes them. "It's my heaven on Earth," Elizabeth says.

OPPOSITE The garden fronts a guest cottage designed to replicate the couple's first home and remind them of their early years together. Fragrant English lavender, edible pineapple guava (*Feijoa sellowiana*), *Agave celsii*, kalanchoe, and kangaroo paws are all evergreen. Their contrasting foliage and flowers provide year-round beauty.

ABOVE Blackberries growing on this fence make it a productive boundary. Elizabeth enjoys the sweet berries while she's on her daily walks through the garden.

OPPOSITE, TOP Elizabeth cuts roses, as well as zinnias, cosmos, *Agastache*, sunflowers, and nasturtiums from her raised beds. The orchard beyond is underplanted with grasses and perennial blooms.

OPPOSITE, LEFT Zach harvests cherry tomatoes.

OPPOSITE, RIGHT A metal arch connecting two raised beds is a vertical design feature as well as functional support for sprawling squash; gold nasturtium and purple basil are a repeated planting in the vegetable garden area that soften the bed edges.

LEFT The garden's entrance provides a vantage point to view the strong geometric design. Chickens, a bunny, and finches in hutches live on one side. Barn cats and honeybees round out the vibrant habitat, and wild creatures visit as well. "Part of a sensory garden has to do with the energy of a space, and nothing brings energy to a space like animals," Elizabeth says. "I love the wild animals that come here. Everything's happily coexisting."

ABOVE A dining table is intentionally set among the growing edibles. This highlights and celebrates the connection between people and plants, soil, and homegrown food. The prominent purple color theme, which includes lavender and *Nepeta*, is very calming for Sophia.

OPPOSITE, TOP A workstation for cleaning veggies and arranging flowers is built in a shaded spot; an adjacent compost bin makes it easy to put trimmings to good use. Elizabeth and Zach love having bouquets made from all that's in season to bring the abundance indoors.

OPPOSITE, BOTTOM Homegrown chamomile, lavender, and honey are healing harvests. Breadseed poppy (*Papaver somniferum*) seedheads are harvested to use in the kitchen too.

takeaway

HOW TO CREATE A SENSORY GARDEN

Your senses are the basis for how you'll experience your garden. Include a range of opportunities to engage all five.

- ▸ **Touch:** To add tactile quality to the garden, use plants such as furry lamb's ears (*Stachys byzantina*); wispy ornamental grasses; papery-petaled flowers such as Iceland poppies (*Papaver nudicaule*) and breadseed poppies (*Papaver somniferum*); roses that form smooth, orb-shaped hips; and coarse, crinkly kale.

- ▸ **Sight:** Adding favorite colors and textures, and contrasting these, provides a visual feast. Incorporate plants such as persimmons, blueberries, maples, and ginkgo, whose leaves change color in the fall.

- ▸ **Scent:** Near patios and paths, situate plants with fragrances that remind you of a place or time, that you find especially energizing or soothing, or that you simply love. Scented geraniums (*Pelargonium*), *Agastache*, and mints all have fragrant foliage. Daphnes, *Osmanthus fragrans*, angel's trumpets (*Brugmansia*), and many others have sweet-smelling flowers.

- ▸ **Taste:** Having favorite fruit, veggie, and herb flavors at your fingertips brings pure pleasure. Grow what you love to eat so you can enjoy it at peak ripeness.

- ▸ **Sound:** Create your own garden soundtrack by using gravel paths that crunch underfoot, adding a burbling fountain, hanging wind chimes, and inviting chirping birds that feed on plant seed heads.

OPPOSITE Dwarf Meyer lemon and succulents are a low-maintenance, water-wise planting above a simple fountain.

Plant medicine

All Courtney Watson wanted was to be able to harvest food from her backyard, but what she got was so much more. A therapist, Courtney had been studying medicinal plants for several years before renovating her garden. Initially, her landscape goals focused on practical features, including chickens and edible crops, but her plans evolved to center on creating a place of healing and personal growth above all else.

"My neighborhood has active gun violence," Courtney says. "Its inhabitants have been historically, and are currently, oppressed, exploited, and intentionally under-resourced, kept away from legitimate and legal means of thriving in our country. That means folx have been forced to turn to less legitimate and 'illegal' means of securing access to resources that ensure their survival and thriving. That comes with violence."

"This is our safe space, and I was very intentional about some of the medicinal plants that we brought in." She added plants known to offer specific spiritual properties, including yarrow for boundaries, borage for courage, and rue, bay, and tobacco for protection.

Experiencing her plants as living beings with agency, Courtney harvests only as much as she immediately needs. She largely relies on her plants' natural life cycles of dropping leaves and flowers, and then uses those in her spirit medicine teas and tinctures. Making these feels instinctual to her, as though she's being guided by ancestors. Past generations of her family grew food, and her garden has brought back a sense of connection with them. "Being with the land was how they made money, how they existed in the world," she says. "Working with the plants for income and making medicine is in my line but hasn't happened for a long time, so when I started working with the plants, I started remembering these old ways."

Courtney is committed to living with her plants in what she learned in her studies as "right relationship"—freely giving and receiving. She often sits in stillness, and when she hears a certain plant calling to her, she holds onto a stem and absorbs the inherent qualities it is offering.

continued

OPPOSITE Courtney's favorite seat in the garden is surrounded by lush plants and shaded in the afternoon. Blueberry, apple, herbs, and medicinal tobacco are grown alongside ornamental plants.

"Learning about my worth is something that the plants have offered to me," she says. "I do a lot in the world, I give out a lot, but I don't necessarily allow people to give back. Because of my work with plants, I'm better with people because I learn to work in true reciprocity: continually knowing that I am among sentient beings that have needs, wants, and desires that I can support, and in turn they will support my needs, wants, and desires. And it's not transactional; it is through love and care that that reciprocity happens."

"Everyone is going to have to find their own way of relationship with the plants," Courtney says. "If you sit and listen, and know that there are beings around you that have gifts to offer and you are willing and able to receive your gifts, then what that looks like in relationship is up to you. And also, don't feel weird about doing weird shit because nobody can see you."

While Courtney got the chicken coop and edible crops she originally envisioned, the spiritual sustenance from her garden has been an unexpected blessing. "I got protection, I got ease, I got peace," she says. "My garden has allowed me to see more of myself. I feel so honored to continue to be in reciprocity with these plants, to pour love onto them, and even when I'm not actively engaged with them just to watch them thrive and grow."

OPPOSITE, RIGHT Courtney spends time visiting with each plant, including yarrow and rose which are both important medicinal perennials.

ABOVE This 27 by 14-foot backyard is packed with a seating lounge, space for edible and medicinal crops, a chicken run, and a dedicated kid fun area in the side yard. An L-shaped raised bed holds a variety of herbs, flowers, and vegetables. In the center, a 'Santa Rosa' plum brings vertical interest; it's underplanted with evergreen *Leucadendron* 'Ebony', *Asparagus densiflorus* 'Myers', and *Aloe* 'Blue Elf'. Digiplexis 'Illumination Flame' and medicinal yarrow provide cutting flowers.

THIS PAGE Courtney steeps nasturtium, roses, and other flowers for their floral essences without cutting off the blooms so that she does less harm to the plants. "I think that everything has a life, everything grows and dies, and you know and honor that," Courtney says. "You treat life the way you want your life to be treated," she says. To give back to her plants, Courtney offers smoke from handmade cigars of *Nicotiana tabacum* leaves and plays music. "Sometimes it's not so much what you're doing as the intention behind it," she explains. "Just the gift of being able to see that they are knowing, they are feeling, that I can acknowledge their sentience and offer a gift on top of that, is everything."

OPPOSITE A container grouping includes 'Bearss' lime, culinary sage, succulents, mullein (*Verbascum*), alyssum, *Artemisia* 'Powis Castle', and *Nicotiana tabacum*.

takeaway

MAKE THE MOST OF
A COMPACT SPACE

You can pack a lot of experiences into a smaller garden by following these tips.

- ‣ Create a central planting area with a perimeter path that circulates traffic around it. This gives a feeling of spaciousness, with plenty to explore every step of the way.

- ‣ Add a fruit tree or other tall element, such as garden art, in the central planting space. This creates visual dimension beyond the ground-level plane.

- ‣ Integrate side yards. These typically long, narrow spaces are often forgotten, but they're valuable real estate. Multi-use side yards can provide space for a hammock, a chicken run, a kids' play area, or a viewing garden.

OPPOSITE, TOP AND BOTTOM LEFT In a side yard, Courtney grows angel's trumpet (*Brugmansia*), medicinal passion flower (*Passiflora caerulea*), white mugwort (*Artemisia lactiflora*), calendula, and other shade-tolerant medicinal plants.

OPPOSITE, BOTTOM RIGHT Courtney makes tea steeped with mullein and yarrow.

Fredrika finds that some pieces are too powerful for her indoor space, such as this painting by Senegalese visual artist Aly Kourouma, but they look right at home among the backyard nature. She protects the art with a sealant used on outdoor murals and brings the work inside when it rains.

Beauty as a balm

Contemplating her plant- and art-filled backyard, Fredrika Newton says, "It's a life force. This garden is so restorative to me, it feels medicinal. I specifically look out here in order to focus and bring calm or to regulate my mood—everything out here contributes to an overall sense of peace, and I am finding that I've grown to really relish that feeling."

As president and cofounder of the Dr. Huey P. Newton Foundation, which is dedicated to maintaining the mission and promoting the true legacy and history of the Black Panther Party and its eponymous cofounder, Fredrika explains the complex nature of the work she and her team are doing. Whether coordinating to rename a street, creating a public art installation, or exploring the development of a multi-site national park to commemorate the Party, she says, "We make sure the history is accurate and accessible to folks. The Black Panther Party was an international organization, but there are people in the city where it was born that don't know the history. These young men and women in the Party were freedom fighters and out of love for their community were willing to sacrifice a lot. It really was love that propelled these people to make the sacrifices that they did. And people don't know that history."

Every work day, Fredrika looks onto her backyard through the windows in her home office. When reimagining the space, she says, "I needed some light, I needed spiritual food, I needed tranquility, I needed a place of respite. Home is really important to me, so I didn't want to have to leave my home in order to get it. I wanted it to be provided for me here. This is what I look at all day long, and it inspires me to do the work that I'm doing."

The garden design blends influences: lacy textures lend a ferny, meditative retreat mood; plants and hardscape reflect contemporary California; and flowers and foliage evoke a balmy, almost tropical Southern style that feels like home to Fredrika.

continued

Art is part of the fabric of Fredrika's life, and it's a big component of her garden as well. She especially loves supporting local and Black emerging artists, and she fills her home with a curated collection that extends into the outdoors. Some pieces, including totems, stone sculptures, and bird baths, adorn the garden throughout the year, and she brings other pieces outside seasonally. In support of this creative space, the planting design is intended to inspire, pairing art with the dynamic energy of seasonal flowers, foliage, and edibles as well as with birds, butterflies, and other pollinators. "Art inspires me to do the work that I do—I get ideas that are outside the box," she says. "Art gives me courage to think creatively in ways that I might not ordinarily or felt like I had the permission to do."

Incorporating food was important too. Fredrika says, "To actually have food growing in my own garden is huge." Fruiting shrubs and trees include 'Bearss' lime, Meyer lemon, blueberries, peach, 'Fuyu' persimmon, pineapple guava (*Feijoa sellowiana*), culinary bay, and elderberry, along with herbs such as rosemary and mint and a planter filled with seasonal veggies.

Noting the succession of flowers, foliage, and edibles that arrive throughout the year, Fredrika says, "This has been life changing for me, to have this amount of beauty. This is the biggest gift I've given myself in a long, long time. It's the gift that keeps on giving because it changes every day."

OPPOSITE, LEFT Fredrika commissioned a large decorative structure to help create privacy. *Farfugium japonicum* var. *giganteum* hugs its base; behind it, bamboo and other tall plants add screening. Viewing the garden "is like looking at a beautiful painting every day that changes before your eyes," she says.

OPPOSITE, RIGHT Tiles created by artist Rose Hill form the surface of the coffee table.

LEFT This bird bath was made by an artist at the Creative Growth Art Center, a non-profit organization that advances the inclusion of artists with developmental disabilities. Feathery *Acacia cognata* Cousin Itt gives it an evergreen frame.

BELOW A mother-and-child sculpture is framed by burgundy-leaved Jazz Hands Bold loropetalum, roses, *Trachelium caeruleum*, Peruvian lily (*Alstroemeria*), ground orchid (*Epidendrum*), variegated hydrangea, 'Swane's Golden' cypress, honeybush (*Melianthus major*), and giant bird of paradise (*Strelitzia nicolai*).

Layers of foliage texture
give the garden a soothing
atmosphere. The backyard
is a peaceful, breathing
space that feels expansive
when Fredrika entertains,
but is cozy when she needs
a private retreat.

ABOVE, LEFT Roses (Frida Kahlo rose is pictured) remind Fredrika of her mother's rose garden.

ABOVE, RIGHT A shady fence line is made productive by incorporating hydrangea for cutting and a Black Tower elderberry with spring flowers that are perfect for a refreshing cordial or dessert syrup. Its fall berries can be made into a medicinal syrup. The apple tree reminds Fredrika of her late father who tended an apple tree in her childhood garden.

OPPOSITE Drapey Kashmir cypress, burgundy rubber plant, and *Asparagus densiflorus* 'Myers' surround a secluded lounging spot.

THIS PAGE "I wanted to plant food that I really enjoy," Fredrika says, and her favorites include peaches and green beans. "I find the fruits and vegetables I've grown, and that I cook and bake with, just taste better to me, and they're very central to my diet. 'Garden to table' was something I was striving to do, and I couldn't be happier with what I've been able to create for myself."

OPPOSITE A 'Bearss' lime to the left and culinary Bay laurel (*Laurus nobilis*) to the front right provide evergreen framing for a focal point totem. Roses, bougainvillea, *Trachelium caeruleum*, Peruvian lily (*Alstroemeria*), Digiplexis, and bronze-leafed canna add long-season color and cutting blooms.

takeaway

PLACE MEANINGFUL ITEMS IN THE GARDEN

Items that hold meaning for you, such as framed art; wood, metal, or ceramic sculpture; or other outdoor-friendly pieces can make your garden even more special. Here's how to highlight them.

- ‣ Give meaningful pieces a consistent backdrop. This could be a painted fence, a solid swath of evergreen plants, or other uniform, neutral plantings that allow your art or other works to shine.
- ‣ Place major pieces within sight lines, such as at the end of pathways, where they'll be easily and regularly seen.
- ‣ For more intimate experiences, tuck small pieces such as bird baths or vessels into plantings so you'll see them while strolling along paths and up close.

seven

Gathering wonderlands

Yes, food, flowers, and so much more that matters are included in this chapter's gardens. But, at heart, they are places to be and to connect—with yourself, with your friends and family, or with your larger community. These gardens inspire us to sit a little longer and commune with loved ones, and they help us to hold memories of time well spent too.

OPPOSITE Gimlet cocktails are flavored with lavender and garnished with cucumbers, both harvested fresh from the garden.

Good to gather

"We are all about entertaining," says Marcy Segre, who, with her husband, Dave, loves welcoming guests to their home. An inviting outdoor gathering space was a must-have—but the catch was that the most accessible area for this was their bigger-than-usual side yard, which also housed trash bins, an air conditioner, and other utilities.

To transform the utilitarian pass-through into a welcoming lounge, fencing and lattice were added to obscure the utilities. This allows a captivating collection of plants, layered from ground level up to small trees, to steal the show. Because the garden is used all year long, it includes plants that peak in different seasons and thrive in shifting light conditions. Foliage and flowers create a rhythmic pattern, drawing the eye down the corridor. "You're entering this space that's very private and very serene," Marcy says. "It's so lush and green, it feels like you're walking into this other wonderful world."

Personal touches are woven throughout. Dwarf Southern magnolias, sago palms, and leopard plants (*Farfugium japonicum*)—all used in showcase gardens of the South—are a nod to Marcy's Georgia roots. Dwarf Italian cypress, boxwood, and shade-tolerant roses—found in traditional Italian gardens—reflect Dave's Italian heritage. Dave also collects art and loves being able to display favorite pieces to enjoy every time they're in the garden.

Dave uses both the side and front yards for daily tea breaks, phone calls, and reading the paper, delighting in the variety of birds that visit. "It's enriching and calming," Dave says. "The only other time my head clears like that is when I bike ride."

As someone who didn't consider herself a gardener and now spends part of every day tending, harvesting, and being in her landscape, Marcy says, "It makes me so happy. Being out with the plants really makes me feel the seasons and feel connected to the natural world. It just feels like this magical space."

OPPOSITE Around a focal point bench, *Hydrangea arborescens* 'Annabelle', angel's trumpet (*Brugmansia*), and Burgundy Iceberg rose add rich colors. Dwarf cypress, magnolia, and beyond, a black-and-white sculpture by ceramist Jun Kaneko add vertical dimension.

ABOVE, LEFT Evergreens, including giant bird of paradise and 'Little Gem' magnolia, create a green room around Marcy and Dave's main gathering space.

ABOVE, RIGHT Fan-shaped *Chamaerops humilis* palm fronds and glossy-leaved 'Little Gem' magnolia provide contrasting evergreen foliage, while the long-blooming, colorful flowers of *Salvia* Mystic Spires Blue support pollinators.

ABOVE, LEFT Shade-tolerant *Farfugium japonicum* var. *giganteum*, 'Old Berkeley' fuchsia, *Chamaerops humilis*, *Aeonium canariense*, peppermint-scented geranium, and giant bird of paradise are a serene palette.

ABOVE, RIGHT 'Sunshine Blue' blueberry grows alongside evergreen *Coprosma* 'Rainbow Surprise', *Aeonium canariense*, and yucca.

RIGHT 'Old Berkeley' fuchsia is a part-shade tolerant bloom.

LEFT "I love to have people over, but I enjoy the garden more for myself," says Marcy, who made flash cards for every plant to learn their botanical names. "I love being out in the garden and working with the plants. They have such special characteristics on display at different times, and it's so fun to see that unfold during the year."

BELOW Low evergreen plantings soften path edges and define spaces in the narrow garden. A consistent color and texture scheme—blue, green, orange, and gold foliage, along with swordlike and grassy forms—is used throughout.

OPPOSITE In this narrow space, layered plants create the illusion of depth. Strappy textures and columnar tree forms are situated rhythmically to guide the eye through the space.

takeaway

USE FLOWERS THAT
BRIDGE SUN AND SHADE

Most gardens have a mix of sun and shade. It can be challenging to find flowers that bridge those exposures, but over the years I've found that some plants labeled as sun lovers will also do well in less light, which helps establish a cohesive floral color palette across the landscape. Here are my favorites that will bloom in part sun/part shade.

- Angel's trumpet (*Brugmansia*)
- Burgundy Iceberg and 'Iceberg' roses
- Digiplexis
- Fuchsia
- Geum
- Hydrangea (pictured right)
- Peruvian lily (*Alstroemeria*; pictured right)
- *Salvia* 'Indigo Spires' and Mystic Spires Blue

OPPOSITE, TOP Marcy also wanted to grow food with their kids. Because the rest of the property was more shaded, it worked best to situate most of their edible crops in raised beds in the sun-soaked front yard. A wide central pathway is welcoming and in scale with the house and landscape.

OPPOSITE, BOTTOM LEFT The front yard is planted with an array of fruit trees and pollinator-attracting blooms that can be used for cutting. It's a haven in it's own right and Dave likes to sit out and read on the front steps.

OPPOSITE, BOTTOM RIGHT Marcy harvests culinary herbs and flowers (golden sage, sunflowers, and basil are shown) for seasonal bouquets.

Community jewel

Beauty matters to Nwamaka Agbo and Misha Balmer, and it's something they wanted not only for themselves, but also to share with family, friends, and neighbors. Their neighborhood was once a thriving part of their city but has declined due to public disinvestment and neglect over the years. Where they live, access to shared green space is limited, and that's partly what motivated them to create a vibrant landscape to enjoy along with their community.

The compact front garden is designed with both clear boundaries and openness. A casual social spot, it's a jewel box of sensory gems that look stunning all year, enjoyed by neighbors who pass by and warmly welcoming to Nwamaka and Misha every time they come home. Behind the house, their outdoor lounge offers ample, and flexible, seating for different sized gatherings. It is a setting for solitary rest and relaxation, business meetings, and festive, soul-filling parties. Nwamaka, the CEO of a foundation focused on restorative economics, explains that her work requires a lot of focused thinking, and their garden sanctuary offers both stillness and the expansiveness to dream. "The ability to have space that's beautiful but still rooted in community is important for the work that I do," she says.

In both front and back gardens, layers of colorful, textural, fragrant flowers, along with grasses, shrubs, and small trees, create an immersive plant experience. Misha says that motorcycles, fireworks, and helicopters all contribute to ambient sounds in their neighbor-hood, and being able to connect with nature in their garden helps balance out the noise. "It makes you wish that for everyone."

He adds that the visiting urban wildlife drawn to their garden, including cats, bunnies, and chickens, along with the sustenance of their plants, helps them slow down and stay grounded. "Living in an urban area, people are close together—that affects the psyche, and we take for granted how important nature is for healing," he says. "It feels good to do something beautiful in a space that feels forgotten, and use the outdoor area in a way that gives energy back."

OPPOSITE Nwamaka and Misha wanted a garden that the neighborhood could enjoy. "You usually have to leave our part of the city to have this type of beauty," Nwamaka says.

ABOVE A low, open-slatted fence creates a gentle boundary and sense of enclosure, while allowing passersby to enjoy the garden. Contrasting evergreens, including *Leucadendron* 'Ebony', are triangulated to guide the eye through the space. Blueberries (to the left) add fall foliage color.

OPPOSITE, TOP Evergreen blueberry and avocado partner with pollinator-attracting *Salvia* Mystic Spires Blue and a strappy plum-colored cordyline for a striking visual display.

OPPOSITE, BOTTOM Edible taro (*Colocasia esculenta*) reflects Nwamaka's Nigerian heritage.

RIGHT Winter-blooming 'Pink Mink' protea makes a great cut flower.

BOTTOM LEFT A mix of evergreens, flowering perennials, and an edible banana (*Musa acuminata*) line the path leading to the garbage enclosure.

BOTTOM RIGHT Evergreen 'Lavender Lady' mangave plays off *Leucadendron* 'Ebony' and variegated New Zealand flax.

BELOW Evergreen *Adenanthos sericeus,* New Zealand flax (*Phormium*), pineapple guava (*Feijoa sellowiana*), giant bird of paradise (*Strelitzia nicolai*), and *Agonis flexuosa* 'Jervis Bay Afterdark' soften the foundation of the house. Edible taro (*Colocasia esculenta*) and an apricot (to the right along the fence) offer harvest.

OPPOSITE, TOP LEFT Reflecting Misha's Japanese and Russian roots are, 'Fuyu' persimmon (pictured), ume (*Prunus mume*), kumquat, and yuzu (*citrus junos*), a gift from Misha's mom.

OPPOSITE, TOP RIGHT Nwamaka loves flowers including this Angel Face rose.

OPPOSITE, BOTTOM Dwarf culinary bay (*Laurus nobilis* Little Ragu) and *Agave desmetiana* are mid-level evergreens that soften the fence. A fig is espaliered to maximize space and highlight the weathered boards behind it. Nwamaka prefers to host friends outdoors rather than inside. "I love a good backyard party," she says. "I can be here with my friends and be loud and crazy while Misha's inside watching football."

ABOVE Clumping bamboo is an evergreen backdrop. Low-growing New Zealand hair sedge (*Carex testacea*) and *Graptoveria* 'Fred Ives' soften the edges of crushed-gravel paving. A small lawn offers flexible space for lounging and gathering. Fruiting ume plum and persimmon trees provide verticality.

Misha and Nwamaka planted an ume tree (pictured left) to use in traditional Japanese recipes including umeboshi (pickled plums, pictured top right) and umeshu (Japanese plum liqueur) that Misha grew up with. He makes these with his mom, Satsuki May Balmer, which has helped him cultivate a deeper, more meaningful connection with his heritage.

takeaway

FAVORITE FRONT YARD FRUIT TREES

A beautiful front yard is a gift to yourself and to anyone who passes by. To get the most utility from your garden, include some fruit trees. Keep in mind that not all fruit trees are created equal, and some grow with a form that is much more attractive and tidy than others. Here are a few of my favorite deciduous fruit trees for the front yard. (Note: If planting trees with soft fruit, such as plum, pluot, and apricot, site them away from driveways or walkways, because falling fruit can stain these surfaces.)

- ‣ Apple
- ‣ Apricot
- ‣ Pear (pictured above)
- ‣ Persimmon
- ‣ Plum
- ‣ Pluot
- ‣ Quince

Commune in the city

At the start of each day, the first thing Rose Thomas does is throw open the kitchen doors leading to her backyard garden, inviting in the crisp morning air and birdsong, dissolving the lines between indoors and out. For Rose and her husband, Jerry, the backyard is a manifestation of the couple's main intentions: caring for nature, cultivating community, and teaching their young son, Axel, to do the same.

Initially, the backyard was a blank slate with just a few mature trees. Rose was committed to keeping them, even though it meant their garden would have less sun exposure because of shade cast by the trees' leafy canopies. "The trees were here before us, and we need to honor them," Rose says. "Despite being a descendant of white settler colonialists, I feel a deep kinship with living things. As a child, trees were my friends—I had this one tree I would always talk to. And in my bones, caretaking is fundamentally part of my spirituality, the responsibility of stewarding land to the best of your ethical ability as a human being."

The family is in the garden every day—watering, harvesting, and playing on the small patch of lawn, usually barefoot. Axel explores every inch as his own wild playground. The space is integral to how they live, and they regularly welcome others for afternoon tea or wine, weekly pizza-and-movie nights, and longer stays in the accessory dwelling unit (ADU) they built specifically to house not only visiting family and friends, but also a wider community of artists and makers who share their values. The garden's design provides both privacy and separateness from the ADU and serves as a gathering space and bridge between the ADU and the family's home. "Community is deeply important to us," Rose says. "Our family is bigger than just our blood."

The feeling Rose and Jerry strove to create was one of abundance in terms of food, friendship, and a well-loved natural space. Ultimately, they aim to model for Axel the answer to several important questions: "In the time that we live in this house, what is our responsibility to the other living things that we're in relationship with?" Rose asks. "And how do we make it better, how do we leave it better than it was?"

OPPOSITE Tucked amid evergreens, seasonal blooms of Digiplexis 'Illumination Flame', native Western columbine (*Aquilegia formosa*), *Salvia* Mystic Spires Blue, and *Nigella* brighten a decomposed granite path at the rear of the yard. Lime-green colored Eastern redbud (*Cercis canadensis* 'Hearts of Gold') are triangulated through the space.

OPPOSITE, TOP A galvanized metal trough for annual edibles and flowers is accessible from the path. The other side is obscured from the rest of the garden by a mix of evergreens and perennial bloomers. Evergreen *Pittosporum*, cordyline, and *Podocarpus* are situated along the fence line and will grow to be an evergreen backdrop.

OPPOSITE, BOTTOM Rose, Jerry, and Axel love the small lawn that provides flexible space for play, picnics, sky-gazing, and more.

RIGHT Since full sun is scarce on the property, the raised vegetable beds are placed in the sunniest spots of the side yard entry and backyard. Sage, purple basil, French marigold, and strawberry soften the raised bed edges.

BELOW The sunny side yard has space for tomatoes, as well as a fig and an everbearing raspberry (*Rubus idaeus* 'Heritage') that are trained along cables attached to the house. A vintage sink with a work surface is ideal for washing off crops.

The couple's priority was to create flexible, usable space for their family and community. A wooden deck was built at the same level as the interior flooring, with enough space for Rose and Jerry to step outside for morning coffee or afternoon lemonade, while Axel plays with his trucks. Wide stairs serve as stadium-style seating for casual get-togethers with other families.

TOP LEFT Rose and Axel harvest alpine strawberries (*Fragaria vesca*) together from a shady spot in the rear of the garden. Rose spent several years working on small farms, and growing food for her family was a priority, as was including native plants, wildlife, and pollinators. "I'm not a city person at heart, so this is my compromise for living in the city: making it as natural and farming focused as possible," she says. "For me, joy and peace is natural space."

TOP RIGHT The outdoor dining space will be shaded by the deck-side persimmon tree, from afternoon into evening, when it's full grown. A potted 'Bearss' lime is just outside the kitchen door for easy harvest.

RIGHT Rose revived this jade plant that once belonged to her maternal grandmother and has kept it in her grandmother's pot.

takeaway

A SEAT FOR ONE, A SEAT FOR ALL

Plan your outdoor space around your daily life and to allow for different types of gatherings—whether hosting a weekly pizza night with friends, sipping morning coffee with your partner, or just enjoying quiet time with the birds. Think intentionally and aim for flexibility in furnishings and permanent layout choices to make your garden a space that supports it all.

▸ Make it easy to be in your garden every day. Right outside your back door—a spot that's easy to get to and use on a daily basis—is ideal for a pair of comfortable club chairs or a small bistro table and chairs where you can have morning coffee or afternoon tea.

▸ Farther away, where you're cocooned in plants that you placed around the perimeter, set a comfy chair for reading or solo contemplation.

▸ When selecting furniture, opt for lightweight pieces when possible. Being able to move things easily will offer more flexibility when you want to modify the setup for different group sizes.

▸ Use stools as side tables, which can double as extra seating as needed.

▸ If you have stairs, make them wider than standard, as the Thomas family did, so that they can serve as informal seating at bigger parties and neighborhood movie nights. Set up retaining or accent walls with a wide cap at a height that can provide comfortable seating.

▸ A small patch of grass, water-wise groundcovers, or a gravel surface can serve as space for kids to play. Add blankets and pillows for lounging.

Midway through the garden, enveloped by lush greenery, is Christine's favorite spot for birdwatching and reading. Watery blue foliage adds to the serene vibe, with Kashmir cypress placed alongside the house, Clarity Blue dianella and *Agave* 'Blue Flame' in the central planting area, and Icee Blue podocarpus screening the fence.

Paradise found

"We wanted a green sanctuary, somewhere where we could just relax and forget about the world—and here it is," says Christine Bennett, gazing out at her backyard, which is enveloped in lush, leafy foliage and vibrant tropical hues.

Although the Bennetts' home is situated in a developed suburban neighborhood, it feels like a secluded oasis, thanks to layers of foliage obscuring the back fence and neighboring homes to create a peaceful sense of privacy and enclosure. "You're tucked away and feel like you're in your own space," says Ian, Christine's husband of more than fifty years. "It's a getaway from the world, our little solace."

With happy memories of gardening alongside her grandmother and aunt in the Welsh seaside village of Aberdovey, where she's from, Christine wanted to include roses, rhubarb, hydrangea, and geranium that remind her of her childhood and early travels. Ian, who grew up on a family farm in Salisbury Plain, a small hillside village outside of Kingston, Jamaica, recalls being surrounded by vibrant bougainvillea, huge hibiscus hedges, and fields of gerbera daisies that his parents sold to market. All of these plants have a place in their current garden. "The gerberas and hibiscus give me a sense of comfort and belonging," Ian says. "They're my link to where I grew up."

For the most part, Christine's dream landscape looks nothing like the others she's known. "Most of the plants here I was totally unfamiliar with—all the different grasses, leopard plant, philodendron, ferns, palms, aeoniums," she says. "I'm very happy because of the exotic feeling they create. It all adds to a sense of luxurious abundance."

An avid birdwatcher, Christine is delighted that her garden has drawn in many new avian visitors, especially a mockingbird that sits in a particular tree and sings from early morning until late at night. She often starts her day with coffee and binoculars in a favorite chair with a prime view of all the activity. "You really appreciate nature when you're sitting here, with all the birds and the squirrels," she says. "I feel very grateful, happy, content."

ABOVE, LEFT A variety of birds are drawn to the garden.

ABOVE, RIGHT *Agave* 'Blue Flame' and *Asparagus densiflorus* 'Myers' offer evergreen textural contrast.

THIS PAGE Varied foliage textures and colors from tree fern, giant bird of paradise, *Pieris japonica* 'Flaming Silver', *Farfugium japonicum* var. *giganteum*, *Coprosma* 'Marble Queen', and *Chamaerops humilis* create a lively display along the fence. *Iresine herbstii* 'Brilliantissima' foliage and Burgundy Iceberg roses add bursts of vibrant fuchsia.

A curveaceous walking loop helps define and shape the backyard, while making the garden accessible for strolling and maintenance. The couple's grandkids love running along the pathway and playing on a small lawn that was included just for them.

Between the dining table and fence, tree fern, giant bird of paradise, and clumping umbrella bamboo (*Fargesia nitida*) add screening that creates a feeling of retreat. Ian enjoys the garden later in the day when it's warmer, and the couple sometimes eats dinner on the patio. Guests join regularly for tea and brunch. "It's a great source of pleasure," Christine says. "The garden itself has just been a wonderful gift. We hardly need to go on vacation."

CLOCKWISE FROM TOP LEFT Part shade–tolerant flowers in pink and orange include long-blooming roses, hydrangeas, and abutilons for cutting.

ABOVE, LEFT Ian hand-waters gerberas, part of his daily routine. The philodendron was a housewarming gift from friends in 1976, when the Bennetts bought their home. It's still thriving and a much-loved plant in the garden.

ABOVE, RIGHT An apple tree, one of Christine's favorite childhood fruits, is espaliered against the fence.

OPPOSITE A pair of path-side chairs are sheltered by a red Abyssinian banana (*Ensete ventricosum* 'Maurelii') and existing privet. On the left is a hydrangea for cutting, tucked behind evergreen *Fatsia japonica* 'Spider's Web' and *Aeonium canariense*; on the right are Icee Blue podocarpus, *Salvia* cultivars 'Wendy's Wish' and Mystic Spires Blue, and blush dahlias.

takeaway

CREATE A PERIMETER LOOP

Good circulation is what makes a space come alive and allows you to have an interactive, immersive experience with your garden. Taking care of your garden is also much easier when there's efficient ways to move through it. So, when you design your plot, plan a main path that takes you not only from one end to the other, but that loops back and connects with secondary walkways. There is nothing less enticing than a dead-end in a garden or more annoying than realizing that there's no path that will take you where you want to go.

For adults, a looping track-like path can make even the smallest gardens feel expansive. These pathways are perfect places for taking phone calls or a meditative stroll around your garden. For young kids, a border between 2 and 3 feet tall may be at eye level, so playing along a loop nestled between plants is an adventure, with plants and insects to encounter and investigate. Add stopping points and destinations, such as seating areas or focal plants, to provide different ways of connecting with your garden along the path.

Evergreen *Aeonium canariense*, dianella, and mondo grass edge the pathway.

For one and all

During urban walks around their neighborhood, Malaika Dower and her daughter, Lucy, came upon some fruitful discoveries: blackberries bordering a parking lot, cherries in a community park, herbs and figs in a traffic circle, and grapes growing over a fence, with a sign from its owner inviting passersby to help themselves. Foraging fruit where it was permissible became part of their regular adventures. "I was never an outdoorsy person—I'm an urbanite," Malaika says. Discovering that she could harvest edibles directly from the source was so delightful that she wanted to do it at home, where she, her daughter, her husband, Eben, and her mom, Jacqueline, could have fresh fruit at their fingertips.

Initially Malaika simply wanted to grow raspberries along a side fence, but she eventually decided to renovate the entire backyard. Along with using bright colors reminiscent of Guyana, where her family is from, she says, "I had a vision of what I wanted: elegant garden parties, gracious outdoor living, and playing soca [music] or tinkly jazz to get the vibe going."

The once nearly barren plot now overflows with sweet fruit, vibrant flowers (including a Cinco de Mayo rose in honor of Lucy's May 5 birthday), and foliage, and it expands their home's living space, with spots to read, work, dine, nap, relax, and entertain. Malaika explains that the relationship she's cultivating with her garden is in part for her daughter. "You think about the things you want your kids to have core memories of, and I want my daughter to have a core memory of me doing things I enjoy," she says. "I'm already predisposed for this hard work ethic that's about productivity, productivity, productivity, and I'm trying to free her from that and understand you can be productive doing things that you like."

"It doesn't have to be on the grandest of scales, but who's to say I can't have this luxurious, relaxing-feeling lifestyle? I would love my daughter to grow up with a core memory of casual ease and elegance. Yes, we have jobs and we have hard things going on, but there are tiny moments we can enjoy."

continued

OPPOSITE Because outdoor dining is central to the family's life, it's also a key component of the garden design. A weather-resistant rug defines and makes the dining space feel distinct.

In large part, the backyard is Malaika's solitary recharging space. "I didn't expect it to have such an impact on me," she says. "It's truly my sanctuary: my place to have my time and do what I love to do. The garden gives me peace—it's so easeful and calm, and elegant but not at all formal. There's something about being able to have this outdoor moment that has refreshed this idea I have of enjoying life."

Having inherited her mother's entertaining prowess, and to honor her late father's love of a good party, Malaika regularly welcomes guests. "This garden has given me so much inspiration to live this life, I lure people back here with it," she says. "It's been the impetus for a lot of celebration and non-celebration. Everybody who comes is, like, what's the occasion? And I'm, like, life. The occasion is life."

LEFT Malaika delights in harvesting sweet 'Sun Gold' tomatoes.

OPPOSITE A grassy play zone features a triangular cutout planted with a 'Santa Rosa' plum that adds vertical interest toward the center of the garden. Across the path, a columnar apple grows in another cutout. Seating against the house offers additional spots for lounging.

BELOW Lucy has fully embraced the garden's offerings, making her signature "fruitonade"—lemonade mixed with whatever fruit is in season—that Eben and the whole family enjoys.

RIGHT Though the overall space is compact, the backyard lives large, with zones for growing food, dining, lounging, and play. Two 6 by 2-foot galvanized watering troughs provide just enough space for growing annual crops. Passion fruit against the back fence and citrus on the sides will grow to envelop the yard in lushness.

OPPOSITE Annual crops include colorful marigolds, nasturtiums, pinks (*Dianthus*), and zinnias, along with herbs, strawberries, and annual veggies. Golden decomposed granite surrounds the planters. A 'Bearss' lime against the fence is an evergreen backdrop.

ABOVE Malaika intentionally chose edibles that are familiar to her mother to remind her of their life in Guyana. She uses many of the ingredients, including Guyanese wiri wiri peppers and *Hibiscus sabdariffa* (also known as sorrel or roselle), to flavor her Guyanese cooking.

The garden is the site of weekly neighborhood cocktail hours, annual vin d'orange–making parties, and spontaneous gatherings. "It really has become this additional space for . . . everything," Malaika says. "The garden transformed our family's relationship to our home and being at home. I'm set to be forever outside—this is our new lifestyle."

takeaway

INCLUDE A MICRO LAWN

Lawns often get a bad rap, largely because they require a lot of water
and care to look good. Although water-wise lawn options exist, I find
that they're not quite as easy to use or enjoy as traditional types.

Rather than adding a large lawn, or feeling that you have to do away
with one entirely, you can include a micro lawn. The one pictured
above is about 7 by 9 feet, which gives just enough space to relax on.
Including a micro lawn as a small but intentional design feature adds
a sense of cool lushness, creates negative green space, and can break
up an expanse of hardscape.

OPPOSITE This part sun/part shade plant combination features evergreen 'Sunshine Blue'
blueberry, cannas, Digiplexis 'Illumination Flame', *Salvia* Love and Wishes, Jazz Hands Bold
loropetalum, *Lonicera nitida* 'Baggesen's Gold', and medicinal Lemony Lace elderberry.

eight

Cultural wonderlands

Our gardens—whether they are deeply rooted in tradition or intended to grow new ones—can be both treasure chests and cultural incubators, where we bring family stories, ancestral ways, and our own personal values to life. The landscapes in this section encourage us to nurture what matters and practice new ways of being.

OPPOSITE Red Abyssinian banana (*Ensete ventricosum* 'Maurelii')

Suburban wild

Nestled into the end of a suburban cul-de-sac, the front yard of Ron Koo and Miwa Hayashi's home is both subtle and striking. It merges their shared love of modern design with the essence of a native California landscape.

The couple's garden wish list was very personal, representing their geography, culture, and values. Ron longed for a landscape that paid tribute to the Sierra Nevada foothills of his childhood, while honoring Miwa's desire for a streamlined look to harmonize with their home's aesthetic. They both wanted to include edibles that were hard to find at local markets and that reflected Ron's Chinese heritage and Miwa's Japanese roots. And including water-wise plants that could survive on little more than rainwater was a priority, given that their region has faced increasing drought conditions over the years.

To maintain its good looks and welcome Ron and Miwa throughout the year, the garden's design relies on a strong framework of evergreen plants with deep green, silver, and bright lime-green leaves that guide the eye through the space. In the center, hugged by larger plants and obscured from the street, is Ron's meadow-like exploration area, planted with more ephemeral native wildflowers and edible weeds for harvest. Over time, as he's studied different concepts like permaculture and rewilding, Ron has focused on letting go of the reins and inviting nature to manage much of the garden.

Although he does do some pruning and cleanup from time to time, Ron keeps his touch light and describes his relationship with the garden as being experimental. "The garden keeps changing," he says. "I adjust by trying different things as I learn and develop a deeper understanding of our ecosystem."

In the central meadow, evergreen succulent *Senecio mandraliscae* fronts this bed of natives (manzanita, California poppies, and *Penstemon heterophyllus* 'Margarita BOP') and water-wise perennials (*Verbena bonariensis*, pineapple guava, edible Mexican weeping bamboo, and coleonema). A Chinese pistache tree balances a statuesque 'Hercules' aloe tree and provides dramatic autumn color.

LEFT Ron loves being able to harvest some kind of fruit and vegetable virtually year round. "There's an expectation that the freshest foods are the most tasty and good for you," he says. "There's nothing more local than harvesting something from your garden and eating it immediately."

BELOW Dwarf 'Champagne' loquat fruit (pictured left) and edible pineapple guava flowers (pictured right) are part of the spring harvest.

ABOVE Although most of the plants need minimal irrigation, those that produce food or support habitat receive supplemental watering in the drier months from Ron and Miwa's gray water system and their 11,000-gallon tank below the driveway that stores rain runoff. "I grew up in California where drought is normal," Ron says. "As a child, there were times when we could do no outdoor watering at all." A grouping of California native manzanita (*Arctostaphylos*) near the street creates a boundary without requiring a fence or formal hedge.

RIGHT Ron and Miwa grow myoga ginger (*Zingiber mioga*) in a part-shade spot that gets morning sun. Its edible flower buds are used in soup and pickles.

RIGHT Although Ron once actively suppressed weeds, he now sows seed of edible weeds and herbs, including sowthistle, wild mustard, and parsley, for harvesting and lets them reseed naturally as fillers in the garden. "Wild mustard is an ancestor to so many of the mustard greens we eat these days," Ron says. "I can forage in my own garden if I just let things grow."

BELOW Contrasting evergreen foliage colors from succulent *Senecio mandraliscae*, lime-foliaged coleonema, and gold-edged *Agave desmetiana* 'Variegata' support short-lived blooms of native purple *Penstemon heterophyllus* 'Margarita BOP', *Verbena lilacina* 'De La Mina', and California poppies.

ABOVE A loose, natural planting with highly textural edibles and perennials, including rosemary, plum-leaved smoke tree (*Cotinus*), pineapple guava (*Feijoa sellowiana*), loquat, *Verbena bonariensis*, euphorbia, tree aloe (*Aloe* 'Hercules'), and *Calandrinia spectabilis*, softly counters the home's modern architecture.

ABOVE, LEFT Near a cardoon and throughout the garden, Ron lets branches and leaves decompose in place, rather than buying loads of bark as he once did. "It's wonderful mulch," he says. "Nature creates its own rich soil naturally." Recently, when a small tree died, he left it to decompose in place, where it could continue to provide food and shelter for insects. "Everything you see around you is habitat for something," Ron says. "There's a reason nature has its systems. I try not to disturb it too much, because everything represents someone else's home."

ABOVE, RIGHT Ron has developed a pruning method for his 'Fuyu' persimmon to encourage shorter, stronger branches.

LEFT Electric-pink–flowered *Calandrinia spectabilis*, deep green edible Natal plum (*Carissa macrocarpa*), a chartreuse coleonema shrub, 'Fuyu' persimmon, 'Violette de Bordeaux' fig, and candy cane bamboo (*Himalayacalamus falconeri* 'Damarapa') with edible shoots are a colorful approach to the side yard gate.

BELOW Bordering the street, edibles and natives unite, with silver-leaved California fuchsia (*Epilobium septentrionale* 'Select Mattole'), *Agave parryi*, gold coleonema, manzanita, rosemary, *Calandrinia spectabilis*, cardoon, loquat, poppies, and a plum-colored smoke tree (*Cotinus*) to create a soft yet structured look.

INTEGRATE FRUIT TREES INTO A WATER-WISE LANDSCAPE

Fruit trees are integral to any garden wonderland, and in order to produce plentiful and tasty fruit they need regular water. Fortunately, even if you live in a drought-prone area, you can still incorporate fruit trees (and other thirstier plants like cutting flowers and bamboo for harvest and screening) into your landscape.

To do this, it's as simple as setting up multiple irrigation lines: One line will be dedicated to your fruit trees, and any others will go to the rest of your landscape. Keep your fruit trees on their own irrigation schedule so that you can adjust as needed to keep them productive, while maintaining a limited watering schedule for the rest of your water-wise landscape. When you follow the design process outlined in this book, your fruit trees are integrated into your overall garden so they'll benefit not only from their dedicated irrigation line but will also receive supplemental water from the other nearby lines.

Additionally, you may opt to install a gray water system, which captures wastewater from your sink, shower, tub, and washing machine (as long as it doesn't contain human waste or toxic chemicals). You can direct that water to your fruit trees or ornamental landscape plants. If you're interested in a gray water system, make sure you learn about and follow regional requirements and work with a trusted professional.

OPPOSITE 'Fuyu' persimmon foliage contrasts with silvery gray euphorbia and evergreen Mexican weeping bamboo.

Harvesting heritage

Growing up in rural Northern California, Denise Shackleton spent her childhood in a big Italian-American community of family and friends. Her great-grandparents had immigrated from a small Tuscan town, and Denise spent summers watching her grandpa harvest grapes from the vines his parents planted to make into wine. They made the most of the land by hunting, fishing, mushroom foraging, and raising sheep, cows, and pigs—"Just enough to butcher for the family," Denise says. They also tended long rows of tomatoes, peppers, zucchini, and other crops. Most vivid in her mind is the family life centered around communal meals made from scratch and, in summer, her grandma making the most of the abundance—stuffing peppers, zucchini, and zucchini blossoms and canning enough food to fill their pantry for the year.

After living in various places across the country with her husband, Woody, and four now-adult children, Denise says, "I wanted to get back to California and have a garden like my grandfather did." The family eventually settled in a place warm enough to grow the crops of her childhood. In their formal garden, she dedicated an out-of-the-way side yard to growing edibles. "It might have been zucchini flowers that really drove me to have a vegetable garden," she says. "It's one of the things I really like. That was probably the beginning."

Over the course of a decade, Denise removed more and more ornamental trees and shrubs. She swapped them for an abundance of fruit trees, vegetables, and herbs that are important to her Italian heritage and that she grew up eating—including figs, pomegranates, apricots, persimmons, citrus, artichokes, and lots of veggies—so she could harvest year round.

She's also preserving and passing on the strong food culture she grew up with, creating homemade meals from just-picked produce throughout the seasons for Woody, their kids and grandchildren, and her mom, who lives with them. "I didn't realize how much joy I would get out of it," she says. "I get so much satisfaction out of cooking something that's grown out here."

OPPOSITE Denise, with granddaughter Annaliese, grows a meaty oxheart tomato that her family affectionately named "Larry's tomato" because the seed was first saved by her cousin Larry. She's exposing her grandkids to gardening, just as her grandparents did for her, and says, "It's the first thing my grandkids run to when they come over. They want to know what's in the garden and love picking and eating from it."

OPPOSITE, TOP LEFT Squash and their edible blossoms are summer favorites.

OPPOSITE, TOP RIGHT "Larry's tomato" is tucked behind deeply lobed artichoke and broad-leaved rhubarb. Deep burgundy is triangulated along the path with tall New Zealand flax (*Phormium*) and ground-level coral bells (*Heuchera*).

OPPOSITE, BOTTOM Although the landscape maintains its estate style throughout the year, it's filled with an unconventional palette of edibles and cutting flowers. Six 'Fuyu' persimmons are lined up formally in the front yard, a technique usually reserved for ornamental trees. Around the limestone fountain are calamondin citrus, *Leucadendron* 'Ebony', *Aeonium* 'Sunburst', iris, and milkweed.

ABOVE An heirloom grape press from Denise's grandparents' vineyard is both a front yard focal point and a trellising structure that supports squash (including pumpkins for the grandkids) in summer and fava beans in cooler weather. Lavender 'Provence' and 'Meerlo', *Beschorneria*, *Aeonium canariense*, *Aloe striata*, *Phormium* 'Dark Delight', and *Ficus elastica* add texture and color. Avocado, olive, pineapple guava (*Feijoa sellowiana*), Natal plum (*Carissa macrocarpa*), artichoke, and roses provide harvest.

OPPOSITE The path leading from the front yard to the backyard is bordered by edible Natal plum (*Carissa macrocarpa*), swordlike New Zealand flax (*Phormium*), *Beschorneria*, a fruiting olive, and angel's trumpet (*Brugmansia*).

RIGHT Denise painted watercolor labels for the jams she makes and gives to family and friends.

BELOW Denise's grandma let nothing go to waste. "Everything they grew, they'd eat, freeze, dry, or can," Denise says, and she follows in those footsteps, drying bushels of persimmons to eat all year, pickling, and making an abundance of jam, much of which she gives away. Favorites include jalapeño-persimmon, pineapple guava, Meyer lemon–ginger marmalade, and three kinds of tomato jam—one is shown below atop goat cheese, along with fresh and dried fruit from the garden.

LEFT Prehistoric-looking *Tetrapanax papyrifer,* cherry laurel, and 'Swane's Golden' cypress form a backdrop, with fruiting pomegranate, electric-pink *Calandrinia spectabilis,* and orange lantana planted below. Sour Italian 'Chinotto' orange trees and roses line one side of the pool. Cordyline, *Lotus berthelotii, Calibrachoa* Million Bells, succulents, and sweet potato vine (*Ipomoea batatas*) spill from formal containers.

BELOW A fall harvest of pomegranate, pineapple guava, eggplant, and pepper. To keep up with the bounty, Denise has help with maintenance and harvesting and loves cooking from the garden just as her grandmother did. When summer is in full swing, she makes eggplant parmesan, eggplant lasagna, caponata, zucchini bread, soups, and decadent salads. "There are points in the year when everything on our plate is from the garden, and I love that," she says.

ABOVE Though nearly all a similar shade of green, the varying leaf shapes and textures of rhubarb, 'Eureka' lemon, *Aeonium canariense*, *Asparagus densiflorus* 'Myers', and creeping fig keep things visually interesting. *Iresine herbstii* 'Brilliantissima' adds vibrant color without blooms.

LEFT "Everyone of my generation remembers my grandma's cooking so much," says Denise, pictured with her mom, Verna Richardson. "Just those memories, the garden, and cooking keep me connected. My grandma was a big entertainer and would always have big dinners, I aspire to do that too." To preserve her family's culinary history, Denise made a cookbook with many recipes in her mom's and aunt's handwriting.

takeaway

PLANT FOR SUCCESSIONAL FRUIT HARVESTS

When selecting fruit trees for your garden, plant a range of types that will provide fruit to pick throughout the year. Start with what you love—perhaps delicious plums or peaches, which are both stone fruits that are ready to harvest in summer. From there, add apples, pears, or pineapple guavas for autumn; persimmons, pomegranates, or citrus for winter in warmer climates; and loquats, cherries, or blueberries for spring.

If you favor a particular kind of fruit and have space for several trees, plan for a longer, more manageable harvest of that fruit rather than a glut all at once. For example, if you love apples, instead of planting three of a single favorite variety that will ripen at the same time, choose three varieties that each produce fruit at different times of the season (early, mid, and late) so you have a succession of different apples to harvest.

I am always careful to take this approach with family-favorite fruit trees such as apples, mandarins, peaches, and plums. Check online sources to determine the fruiting times of available varieties. For example, the 'Katy' and 'Blenheim' apricot trees pictured above offer an early-season and mid-season harvest, respectively, with fruit production from May through July.

Planting roots

During her childhood in Missouri, Sara Perlitch got her first taste of growing edibles through a friend's dad, who raised crops on a half acre of fertile bottomland. She saw how he not only fed his family from his fields, but the way he shared and traded produce as well. Sara helped harvest and was always welcome to take home some of the bounty, which is top of mind when she gathers crops such as tomatoes, green beans, and lemons from her front and back gardens for her family and others.

When she envisioned her own landscape, she says, "I didn't want any plants that didn't do something." So, rather than have a garden that's simply ornamental and static, she explains, everything had to earn its place by providing something to eat, smell, or see throughout the seasons.

A selection of her plants pay homage to her Russian Jewish heritage. In front, dwarf Russian sage (*Perovskia* 'Little Spire'), wine-colored sanguisorba blossoms, and buttery yellow yarrow (*Achillea millefolium* 'Hoffnung') represent blooms that might be found in a *dacha* garden (edible and medicinal plots at rural, seasonal homes in Russia). In the backyard, a windmill palm (*Trachycarpus fortunei*), common myrtle (*Myrtus*), two types of willow, and etrog citron (*Citrus medica*) represent plants traditionally used in Sukkot holiday festivities that Sara observes every year to celebrate the harvest and shelter. These are viewable from Sara's back patio and help her hold gratitude for the abundance around her. From that spot, surrounded by birdsong, enveloped by floral scents, and watching bees at work, she says her favorite part of having this garden is simply being able to sit outside in the morning with a cup of coffee in peace and take it all in, and adds, "It makes me feel like all's good in the world."

The backyard space is divided into sections that are easily accessed by a decomposed granite path. Raised wooden beds overflow with Sara's favorite edibles. An apricot, blight-resistant 'Bartlett' pear, 'Anna' apple, citrus, and 'Santa Rosa' plum are integrated into the landscape. Perennials including roses and pinks (*Dianthus*), both of which have edible petals, provide seasonal color.

RIGHT Sara grows windmill palm (*Trachycarpus fortunei*), common myrtle, willow, and etrog citron (*Citrus medica*) for Sukkot festivities.

BELOW "My kids and I have a European sensibility about eating, meaning we don't eat junk food or a lot of prepared food," Sara says. "We like to eat vegetables and cook them ourselves instead of buying premade."

ABOVE, LEFT Sara spent a good part of her life working in and traveling to Japan, a country that's very meaningful to her, and she includes Japanese ingredients like shiso, wasabi, and shishito peppers in her garden. Because shade-loving wasabi can be invasive, it is grown in a gray felt grow-bag along the shady entry corridor.

ABOVE, RIGHT Edible purple-tinged 'Opera' artichokes and *Salvia* 'Wendy's Wish' are perennials that provide seasonal color and harvest.

TOP LEFT Sara keeps bees, which have been ultra-productive. "If we never get another drop of honey, I could make it to the end of a very long life with what we have," she says.

BOTTOM LEFT Sara loves observing the landscape's daily changes: "It's nice to have a yard that draws you out instead of one you just walk past."

ABOVE Colorful foliage—green citrus, avocado, and culinary bay; silvery pineapple guava (*Feijoa sellowiana*), fruiting olive, and palm (*Chamaerops*); and burgundy-colored Chinese fringe flower (*Loropetalum*) and coral bells (*Heuchera*)—forms an evergreen framework that keeps the front yard looking good all year. A weeping mulberry tree (rear right) reminds Sara of her childhood.

OPPOSITE *Lomandra*, fruiting olive, citrus, and culinary bay laurel (*Laurus nobilis*) provide an evergreen textural backdrop for seasonally blooming purple *Verbena bonariensis* and deep pink *Grevillea* 'Superb'. "I like coming out and seeing a pop of color that wasn't here yesterday and may not be here tomorrow," Sara says.

ABOVE, LEFT Deciduous 'Jubilee' blueberries are tucked among evergreen grasses in the front yard.

ABOVE, RIGHT An evergreen combination shows off foliage color and texture, with burgundy-leaved coral bells (*Heuchera*); silver-blue pineapple guava and palm (*Chamaerops*) ; and bright green *Lomandra* Breeze, citrus, and culinary bay.

USE COLOR AS A GUIDE ALONG A PATH

To turn a walkway into a more inspired experience, use plants in repeating colors to create rhythm at the ground level. You can do this with a single repeated plant, which is easiest, or choose different plants in the same color if, for example, the path moves from sun to shade and you need options for different exposures, or if you just want more variety. Pictured left, burgundy loropetalum, mauve *Echeveria* 'Afterglow', and plum-colored coral bells (*Heuchera*) at intervals along both sides of the path guide people on their way and elevate what could be a mundane experience into something more beautiful.

Deeply rooted

Each day, my morning walk ends in my backyard wonderland with a daily ritual of delighting in—and giving thanks for—everything my garden has to offer. Enveloped by flowering vines climbing overhead, dramatic foliage blurring the property lines, and beds packed with fruit trees and other edibles in every season, I'm truly blown away by the newest things that are happening. At any moment, it's never quite like it was before, and I'm awed by these moments of beauty that I couldn't anticipate because they're always whatever nature has in store.

As a designer, I wanted a lot from my landscape: raised beds, a grassy patch and play space for my kids, a couch to relax on, a dining table, and a spectrum of plants that I'd been coveting for years as well as others that celebrate our heritage. I intended every inch to overflow with colorful, textural, fragrant elements to light up the senses and support me and my family.

Integral to the garden are plants that reflect my cultural roots: my father is from Jamaica as is my children's father, Linval Owens; my mother is from England; and I grew up in California's Bay Area. So, I made a list of all the plants that told the story of my family. My mom always talked about foraging for berries, had roses, and made us rhubarb crumble. My dad and grandma made fevergrass (also known as lemongrass) tea when we were sick. Linval grew up eating garden-grown passion fruit, bananas, and guava. As a child, I picked fresh oranges off my parents' front yard tree and loved the taste of peach cobbler and apple pie. My parents gave us a strong sense of identity, and I really want to be able to carry that on for my children, Samuel and Zeta.

In our garden, I've made it a priority to flesh out my family's cultural heritage, as I've always valued knowing that I come from people, on both sides of my family, whose lives were rooted in traditions,

continued

continued

OPPOSITE Since this spot is east facing and shaded in the afternoon, it's perfect for my lounge area. Enveloped by *Brugmansia* 'Charles Grimaldi', shell ginger (*Alpinia zerumbet*), 'Distant Drums' rose, yucca, *Bougainvillea* Tahitian Dawn, and Icee Blue podocarpus, I can relax, put my feet up and read, take phone calls, and enjoy breaks from work.

special local ways, daily experience, and medicine and foods that they knew how to make for themselves. Going back to plant relationships and practices that my ancestors developed and held has been very grounding for me. Recalling memories from childhood or elsewhere—like the peace I felt when lying on my parents' little backyard lawn or picking fresh plums in the early summer sun—are really clear vignettes of feeling good and knowing that abundance was present and that I liked it. Recognizing those feelings, and taking the active steps to plant and tend to those things for myself, has been an empowering act of self care.

I want my kids to develop an intimate, respectful connection with nature as well. Now, just outside our back door, they get to know bugs, worms, and birds. They experience the seasons as favorite edibles such as passion fruit, Jamaican sorrel (*Hibiscus sabdariffa*), and calamondin ripen and through watching monarchs land on milkweed and swallowtails munch on fennel. They play in a way that's culturally connecting when they build forts with banana leaves and blend guava drinks from our backyard trees. I really want them to grow up having hands-on daily experiences with plants, knowing them the way they know people in their lives—appreciating their quirks, admiring their attributes, and having stories to tell about them. And that has come to be. I believe because Samuel and Zeta are growing up in relationship with plants, they will absolutely be more respectful and caring about our planet—and that feels both purposeful and exciting.

Above all, my backyard is a place of restoration, where I can relax and be myself. My highest aspiration is to have a simpler life, and when I'm in my garden, I feel close to that. This space really is everything I wanted it to be, but almost more important than that is that I took the time to acknowledge what would be good for me and then put my time and resources toward manifesting it. My garden is reflective of me in a way that is healing and joyous and connecting, and it allows me to be in the world as a more connected, healed, and joyous person.

TOP LEFT I love to cut flowers, including these 'Distant Drums' roses, for arrangements.

TOP RIGHT Sampling just-picked fruit at the peak of ripeness is one of my family's greatest pleasures.

LEFT Dapple Dandy pluots are a favorite fruit linked to my Californian roots.

Lush, low-growing *Pittosporum crassifolium* 'Compactum', *Trachelium caeruleum* 'Hamer Pandora', and *Beschorneria* line the entry path. A pomegranate tree provides autumn fruit. Foliage in green, gold, blue, and burgundy creates a high-contrast framework.

ABOVE The outdoor dining area is adjacent to raised beds so I can easily pick crops including squash, sweet basil, and edible nasturtium flowers for a true garden-to-table experience.

CLOCKWISE FROM TOP LEFT Passion fruit, *Hibiscus sabdariffa* (also known as sorrel or roselle), and fevergrass (lemongrass) link to my Jamaican roots.

ABOVE, LEFT Samuel marvels at the corkscrew-like tendrils on his favorite plant, our passion fruit vine.

ABOVE, RIGHT Rhubarb, roses, and elderberry are among the edible and medicinal plants in my garden that reflect my English heritage.

OPPOSITE My compact backyard is divided into different rooms that are clearly defined. Foliage color and forms are repeated to guide your eye through the space. A guava tree shades the dining table. I have a care team tend to most of the plants just once a month so I can focus on harvesting edibles and flowers, which are the things I like to do.

takeaway

LET PLANTS SHINE BY CHOOSING FURNITURE THAT RECEDES

To make one element in your garden stand out, make the other elements fade away. Here, furniture and a structure are functional—black Adirondack chairs, a coordinating charcoal-gray pergola frame with redwood slats, and a simple redwood coffee table—but understated so plants take center stage. With such minimal variety in materials, in dark or natural finishes, these elements visually recede into the background so that the wide and lively variety of plants can shine.

OPPOSITE Tropical foliage of red Abyssinian banana (*Ensete ventricosum* 'Maurelii'), a connection to the lush foliage forms typical of Jamaica, takes center stage above *Beschorneria yuccoides* 'Flamingo Glow', round-leaved *Farfugium japonicum* var. *giganteum*, and nearly white *Echeveria cante*. Feathery papyrus provides foliage contrast among broad leaves. A grapevine growing up an arbor shades my backyard office, while an espaliered fig softens a corner. Thanks to all the evergreen elements, this is a lush but relatively low-maintenance garden.

Gratitude

LESLIE BENNETT

This book is a testimony to the relationships that have supported me over the last fifteen years as I've found my way in the gardens.

First and foremost, my deepest thanks to Julie Chai, my writing (and dreaming!) partner for this book project and friend and collaborator for more than a decade. It's been the greatest gift and comfort to work with someone whose mind and heart I respect so much and whose values and work style are so aligned with my own. Our creative process with this book has been nothing less than transformative for me. I am so thankful for it and for us!

So much love and gratitude to Rachel Weill for taking exactly the beautiful, warm, and authentic photos I dreamed this book would include, and for bringing your full, passionate, honest self to every single shoot and brainstorming session! I appreciate you so much. Thank you also to Linda Peters for showing up so fully for us all at so many photo shoots. You were the secret sauce that made everything better!

To Holly, Lonna, Jessica, Jorge, Rhan, Corazon, and the whole Pine House team: I'm so proud of the gardens and relationships that we've grown together over the last decade. Thank you for being the hearts and minds of Pine House along with me and for being my friends too.

To all the Pine House clients who have supported Pine House over the years, especially those who shared their gardens in this book, thank you for giving me and the Pine House team the space to be creative; thank you for being our community too.

Thanks to our agents, Leslie Jonath and Leslie Stoker, for believing in this project and in us. To our editors, Lisa Regul and Claire Yee, for saying yes to this book and then really being in it with us. To Ashley Lima and Betsy Stromberg for your inspired design. And to Sohayla Farman and the entire Ten Speed team for your commitment and care in making this book.

Lastly, thank you to my friends, especially Clara, Rebecca, Jillian, Kaitlin, and Lin, for being alongside me for all the ups and downs. To my parents, Christine and Ian, for always supporting me so much, in so many ways. And to my bright stars, Samuel and Zeta, for loving me even when this book project kept me away from you.

JULIE CHAI

Leslie Bennett, every part of our collaboration has been grounding, clarifying, and restorative. Thank you for bringing your highest self to our time together each day, and inspiring me to do the same. I am grateful for the nourishing friendship and partnership we've cultivated, and I have the deepest appreciation, admiration, and respect for you. Our work together has felt like magic and lifted me up in every way.

To the Pine House team, I've felt and am grateful for the tremendous care you put into designing, building, and nurturing each of the stunning gardens that bring to life the lessons in this book.

Rachel Weill, you captured the essence of these gardens and were able to highlight not only their beauty, but also their meaning and depth. Thank you for going above and beyond to draw out the best of each one. Linda Peters, you are pure joy, warmth, and kindness, and kept us uplifted through marathon shoots. Reuniting with you was icing on the cake.

Leslie Jonath and Leslie Stoker, you two are the ultimate pros. Thank you for supporting and guiding us from beginning to end. I feel lucky to have had the chance to work with and learn from both of you over so many years.

Lisa Regul, thank you for saying yes! Your wisdom, insights, and thoughtfulness were essential to getting this project off the ground and keeping it on the right track. Claire Yee, many thanks to you, Sohayla Farman, and the Ten Speed team for guiding us through the finish line.

Betsy Stromberg, thank you for translating our early notes and mockups into beauty on the page. Ashley Lima, thank you for creating the book's stunning design. Your spot-on choices elevated everything, and it was such a pleasure to work with you again.

My parents, Phyllis and Hi-Dong, your warmth, endless curiosity, and delight in forging your own paths have shaped every part of who I am. Thank you for showing me how to live deeply and authentically.

My husband, George, and our son, Ellis, both of you are sunshine and rainbows and continually help me grow into the best version of myself. I love you more than everything.

To everyone who welcomed us into your gardens, thank you for sharing your spaces and yourselves with such generosity. This book wouldn't exist without you.

Garden design credits

GARDEN NAME	DESIGN TEAM
Sher	Lonna Lopez (landscape, cutting flower bed, and container design lead), Jessica Comerford (vegetable and annual flower planting), Leslie Bennett
Lin	Lonna Lopez (landscape design lead), Jessica Comerford (annual vegetable and flower planting), Leslie Bennett
Soja	Holly Kuljian (landscape design lead), Jessica Comerford (annual vegetable and flower planting), Lonna Lopez (container design), Leslie Bennett
Johnson	Lonna Lopez (landscape and container design lead), Jessica Comerford and Kelli Schley (annual vegetable and flower planting), Leslie Bennett
Cozadd	Homestead Design Collective (landscape design); Jessica Comerford, Kiera Jaffin, and Kelli Schley (annual vegetable and cutting flower planting); Leslie Bennett
Knowlton	Holly Kuljian (landscape design lead), Jessica Comerford (annual vegetable and flower planting), Leslie Bennett
Nguyen/Poon	Holly Kuljian (landscape design lead), Lonna Lopez (container design), Leslie Bennett
Horn	Christian Cobbs, Holly Kuljian, Caroline Acquistapace, Leslie Bennett
Watson	Lonna Lopez (landscape design lead), Jessica Comerford (annual vegetable, herb, flower, and container planting), Leslie Bennett
Newton	Holly Kuljian (landscape design lead), Jessica Comerford (annual vegetable, herb, and flower planting), Lonna Lopez (container planting), Leslie Bennett
Segre	Holly Kuljian (landscape design lead), Jessica Comerford (annual vegetable, herb, flower, and container planting), Lonna Lopez (container planting), Leslie Bennett
Agbo/Balmer	Lonna Lopez (landscape design lead), Leslie Bennett
Thomas	Caroline Acquistapace (landscape design lead), Jessica Comerford (annual vegetable, herb, and flower planting), Holly Kuljian, Leslie Bennett
Bennett	Holly Kuljian (landscape design lead), Leslie Bennett
Dower	Lonna Lopez (landscape design lead), Jessica Comerford (annual vegetable and flower planting), Leslie Bennett
Koo	Christian Cobbs, Holly Kuljian, Leslie Bennett
Shackleton	Christian Cobbs, Stefani Bittner, Holly Kuljian, Caroline Acquistapace, Lonna Lopez (container planting), Jessica Comerford (annual vegetable, herb, and flower planting), Leslie Bennett
Perlitch	Lonna Lopez (landscape and container design lead), Jessica Comerford (annual vegetable and flower planting), Leslie Bennett
Bennett/Owens	Holly Kuljian (landscape design lead), Leslie Bennett
Cutting flower and starter veggie garden takeaways	Special thanks to Lonna Lopez for sharing her cutting flower garden design techniques with the whole Pine House team and in this book. Thanks to Jessica Comerford for her support with the starter vegetable garden planning list.

About the contributors

Leslie Bennett is a landscape designer and writer based in Oakland, California, who creates gardens that help to nourish us and tell the story of who we are. Raised in the Bay Area and based in Oakland since 2009, Leslie holds degrees from Harvard University, Columbia Law School, and University College London in the fields of environmental justice, land use law, cultural property, and preservation.

Leslie is the founder and owner of Pine House Edible Gardens (www.pinehouseediblegardens .com), an Oakland-based landscape design/build firm that creates aesthetic edible gardens and productive outdoor spaces, and she is co-author of *The Beautiful Edible Garden* (Ten Speed Press, 2013). She and her team create culturally grounded gardens that provide as much visual inspiration as they do organic harvests of food, flowers, and medicinal herbs.

Leslie and the Pine House team's work have been featured in *Architectural Digest*, *Elle Decor*, *Martha Stewart Living*, OprahDaily.com, *Better Homes & Gardens*, *Sunset Magazine*, *Garden Design*, *C Magazine*, *American Gardener*, *New York Times*, *Los Angeles Times*, *San Francisco Chronicle*, and Gardenista.com.

Writer and editor **Julie Chai** has spent her career covering gardening and landscapes and is the editor of *Floret Farm's A Year in Flowers*, *Floret Farm's Cut Flower Garden*, and *Floret Farm's Discovering Dahlias*. Her work has been featured in media including *Martha Stewart Living*, *Better Homes & Gardens*, the *San Francisco Chronicle*, *Gardenista*, HGTV, and *Sunset Magazine*, where she was the senior garden editor. She lives and gardens in Los Altos, California, with her husband and son.

Photographer **Rachel Weill** has spent the last twenty-five years capturing garden, travel, food, and lifestyle images for the publishing and hospitality industries. She loves storytelling through photos and has an energetic dedication to her work. Rachel photographed the books *Succulent Obsession*, *Growing Weed in the Garden*, and *Every Cocktail Has a Twist*, and her work has been featured in magazines including *Martha Stewart Living*, *Conde Nast Traveler*, and *Sunset Magazine*. Rachel loves to grow food and create eclectic foraged bouquets from her home and garden in San Anselmo, California.

Index

A

abutilon, 195
Acacia cognata Cousin Itt, 84, 87, 153
Acer palmatum 'Butterfly', 94
Achillea millefolium. See yarrow
Adenanthos sericeus, 175
Aeonium, 129, 189
A. canariense, 124, 165, 196, 227, 232
A. 'Sunburst', 227
Aesculus californica. See buckeye
African blue basil, 4, 89, 97
Agastache, 89, 134, 141
Agave, 71, 92
A. attenuata 'Kara's Stripes', 95
A. 'Blue Flame', 188, 190
A. celsii, 133
A. desmetiana, 177
  'Variegata', 218
A. franzosinii, 41, 51, 87
A. parryi, 121, 221
Agbo, Nwamaka, 171–72, 177–78
Agonis flexuosa 'Jervis Bay
    Afterdark', 175
Agrostemma, 109, 110
ají amarillo, 67
Akeson, Steve, 113, 116
Aloe 'Blue Elf', 145
A. 'Hercules', 215, 219
A. striata, 227
A. tongaensis 'Medusa', 84
alpine strawberry (*Fragaria vesca*), 186
Alpinia zerumbet. See shell ginger
Alstroemeria. See Peruvian lily
alyssum, 89, 146
amaranth, 20
angel's trumpet (*Brugmansia*), 141,
    149, 162, 169, 229
  'Charles Grimaldi', 3, 245
Anigozanthos. See kangaroo paw
annuals, 16, 19–21. *See also individual*
    plants
apple, 143, 156, 177, 196, 233
  'Anna', 235
apricot, 8, 175, 177, 225, 235
  'Blenheim', 233
  'Katy', 233
Arctostaphylos. See manzanita
Artemisia lactiflora. See white mugwort
A. 'Powis Castle', 146
Arthropodium cirratum, 124
artichoke, 71, 81, 114, 225, 227, 237
arugula, 97

B

Asian pear, 127
Asparagus densiflorus 'Myers', 39, 89,
    145, 156, 190, 232
Aspidistra elatior 'Milky Way', 94
avocado, 127, 172, 227, 239

backyards, 20, 22
Balmer, Misha, 171, 177–78
Balmer, Satsuki May, 178
bamboo, 113, 153, 177
  candy cane, 221
  Mexican weeping, 215, 223
  umbrella, 194
banana, 30, 71, 77, 174, 245
basil, 89, 92, 108, 169, 250
  African blue, 4, 89, 97
  'Genovese', 68
  purple, 97, 134
  'Spicy Globe', 92
  'Wild Magic', 19, 89, 97, 106
bay laurel (*Laurus nobilis*), 83, 101,
    143, 152, 158, 177, 239, 241
beauty, surrounding with, 10
bees, 67, 238
begonias, 101
belonging, sense of, 13
Bennett, Christine and Ian, 188–89,
    194, 196
Beschorneria, 227, 229, 249
B. yuccoides 'Flamingo Glow', 255
birch, 101
birdhouse gourd (*Lagenaria*
    siceraria), 67
blackberry, 51, 134, 201
Black Panther Party, 151
Blechnum 'Silver Lady', 94
blueberry, 53, 71, 92, 141, 143,
    152, 172
  'Jubilee', 241
  'Sunshine Blue', 165, 211
borage, 89, 143
bougainvillea, 158, 189
  Tahitian Dawn, 245
boxwood, 109, 110, 163
breadseed poppy (*Papaver*
    somniferum), 8, 20, 99, 138, 141
Brugmansia. See angel's trumpet
buckeye (*Aesculus californica*), 59
Buddleja. See butterfly bush
butterfly bush (*Buddleja*), 121

C

Calamagrostis 'Karl Foerster', 125
calamondin, 227, 246
Calandrinia spectabilis, 219, 221, 231
calendula, 19, 20, 89, 114, 149
   'Zeolights', 21, 114
Calibrachoa
   Million Bells, 231
   Terra Cotta, 59
California bay (*Umbellularia californica*), 59
California fuchsia (*Epilobium septentrionale* 'Select Mattole'), 221
California poppy, 55, 71, 215, 218, 221
candy cane bamboo (*Himalayacalamus falconeri* 'Damarapa'), 221
canna, 87, 158, 211
cardoon, 221
Carex testacea. See New Zealand hair sedge
Carissa macrocarpa. See Natal plum
Cercis canadensis
   'Hearts of Gold', 39, 181
   'Ruby Falls', 95
Chamaerops, 239, 241
C. humilis, 164, 165, 191
chamomile, 134
cherry, 24, 101, 201
cherry laurel, 231
Chilean guava (*Ugni molinae*), 72, 79, 84, 92
Chinese fringe flower (*Loropetalum*), 239
Chinese pistache tree, 215
Chinese stem lettuce, 74
chrysanthemum, 74
Citrus junos. See yuzu
C. medica. See etrog citron
clivias, 101
coast live oak (*Quercus agrifolia*), 59
coleonema, 215, 218, 221
Colocasia esculenta. See taro
color, use of, 39, 119, 243
columbine, 110, 181
connecting, making space for, 10–11
Coprosma
   'Marble Queen', 39, 191
   'Pina Colada', 39, 94
   'Rainbow Surprise', 125, 165
coral bells (*Heuchera*), 109, 227, 239, 241, 243
cordyline, 172, 183, 231

Cordyline australis 'Torbay Dazzler', 15
corn, 59, 114
cornflower, 4, 83, 89
cosmos, 20, 106, 118, 134
   'Cupcakes Blush', 21
Cotinus. See smoke tree
Cozadd, Hala Kurdi, 101–2, 104, 106, 108
crape myrtle, 121
Creative Growth Art Center, 153
cucumber, 97, 161
Cussonia paniculata. See mountain cabbage tree
cutting flower beds, designing, 109–10
Cydonia oblonga. See pineapple quince
cypress, 153, 162
   dwarf Italian, 163
   Kashmir, 15, 156, 188
   'Swane's Golden', 127, 231
Cyrtomium falcatum. See Japanese holly fern

D

dahlia, 102, 108, 109, 196
daphnes, 141
dara (*Daucus carota*), 108
delphiniums, 109
dianella, 188
Dianthus. See pinks
Digiplexis, 91, 129, 158, 169
   'Illumination Flame', 145, 181, 211
Digitalis. See foxglove
Dr. Huey P. Newton Foundation, 151
dogwood, 121, 125
Dower, Malaika, 201–2, 207–8
dudleya, 87
dusty miller (*Senecio cineraria*), 109

E

Eastern redbud (*Cercis canadensis* 'Hearts of Gold'), 181
Echeveria 'Afterglow', 243
E. cante, 255
echinaceas, 102, 114
edible flowers, 89
eggplant, 97, 104, 231
   'Rosa Bianca', 67
elderberry (*Sambucus nigra* spp. *cerulea*), 51, 131, 152, 156, 211, 252
English lavender, 8, 133
Ensete ventricosum 'Maurelii'. *See* red Abyssinian banana

Epidendrum. See ground orchid
Epilobium septentrionale 'Select
    Mattole'. *See* California fuchsia
Epiphyllum oxypetalum. See Queen of
    the Night cactus
Erigeron karvinskianus. See Santa
    Barbara daisy
espaliers, 44
etrog citron (*Citrus medica*), 235, 236
Euphorbia, 219, 223
    Black Bird, 28
    'Tasmanian Tiger', 87, 124
everbearing raspberry (*Rubus idaeus*
    'Heritage'), 183
evergreens, 42, 44, 49, 51. *See also
    individual plants*

F

Farfugium japonicum. See leopard
    plant
Fargesia murielae. See umbrella
    bamboo
Fatsia japonica 'Spider's Web', 15,
    33, 196
fava bean, 227
Feijoa sellowiana. See pineapple guava
feverfew (*Tanacetum parthenium*),
    102, 181
fevergrass, 245, 251
Ficus elastica, 227
F. nitida, 43, 87
fig, 114, 177, 183, 201, 225, 232, 255
    'Violette de Bordeaux', 221
foxglove (*Digitalis*), 109, 110
Fragaria vesca. See alpine strawberry
front yards, 21, 22, 179
fruit trees
    for front yard, 179
    garden design and, 47–49
    for successive harvests, 233
    watering, 223
    See also individual fruits
fuchsia, 101, 169, 191
    'Old Berkeley', 165
Furcraea macdougalii, 84
furniture, 25, 187, 255

G

garden wonderlands
    annuals in, 16, 19–21, 68
    benefits of, 1
    bridging sun and shade, 169
    color and, 39, 119, 243
    definition of, 7
    designing, 8–13, 15–31, 33–55
    edible flowers in, 89
    flowering perennials in, 129
    foliage contrast in, 38
    fruit trees in, 47–49, 179, 223, 233
    furniture for, 25, 187, 255
    gathering spots in, 25
    hard-working plants in, 34
    on hillsides, 79
    individuality of, 7, 15, 30–31
    layers in, 42–55
    micro lawns in, 211
    pathways in, 26, 199, 243
    placing meaningful items in, 159
    raised beds in, 19–21, 68
    smaller, 149
    starter summer veggie gardens in,
        96–97
    triangulation and, 37
    visual balance and, 34, 36
gathering spots, 25
gaura, 129
Gem marigolds, 106
gerbera, 189, 196
germander (*Teucrium*), 19, 109, 125
geum, 129, 169
giant bird of paradise (*Strelitzia
    nicolai*), 94, 153, 164, 165, 175,
    191, 194
ginkgo, 141
globe amaranth (*Gomphrena*), 109
grape, 46, 71, 106, 201, 255
Graptoveria 'Fred Ives', 177
green beans, 3, 97
Grevillea 'Superb', 241
ground orchid (*Epidendrum*), 153
guava, 245, 246, 252

H

harvest station, 22
Hayashi, Miwa, 215, 217
hellebore (*Helleborus*), 109
Heteromeles arbutifolia. See toyon
Heuchera. See coral bells
H. maxima, 27
hibiscus, 189
Hibiscus sabdariffa, 13, 207, 251
Hill, Rose, 153
hillside plantings, 79
Himalayacalamus falconeri 'Damarapa'.
    See candy cane bamboo
hollyhock, 30, 71, 77, 174, 245
honeybush (*Melianthus major*), 153
honeysuckle, 101
Horn, Elizabeth, 133, 134, 137, 138
hydrangea, 27, 153, 156, 169, 189,
    195, 196
Hydrangea arborescens 'Annabelle', 162

I

Iceland poppy (*Papaver nudicaule*), 20, 141
indigo (*Indigofera*), 118
Ipomoea batatas. See sweet potato
Iresine herbstii 'Brilliantissima', 191, 232
iris, 27, 113, 121, 129, 227
Italian cypress, 163

J

jade plant, 186
Japanese holly fern (*Cyrtomium falcatum*), 15, 33
Jazz Hands Bold loropetalum, 153, 211
Johnson, Judy, 91–92, 95
juniper, 28

K

kalanchoe, 133
kale, 97, 141
Kaneko, Jun, 162
kangaroo paw (*Anigozanthos*), 41, 121, 127, 129, 133
Kashmir cypress, 15, 156, 188
kiwi, 46
Knowlton, Chris, 113–14, 116, 118
komatsuna, 74
Koo, Ron, 215–18, 220
Kourouma, Aly, 150
kumquat, 71, 177

L

Lagenaria siceraria. See birdhouse gourd
lamb's ear (*Stachys byzantina*), 34, 121, 127, 141
lantana, 231
Laurus nobilis. See bay laurel
lavender (*Lavandula*), 121
  English, 8, 138
  'Meerlo', 227
  'Provence', 124, 227
lawns, 211
lemon, 71
  'Eureka', 232
  Meyer, 77, 141, 152
lemon thyme, 68
lemon verbena, 83
leopard plant (*Farfugium japonicum*), 8, 39, 153, 163, 165, 189, 191, 255
Leucadendron, 71, 79
  'Ebony', 145, 172, 174, 227
lime, 113
  'Bearss', 146, 152, 158, 186, 207
Limonium, 129
L. perezii. See sea lavender
Lin, Karen and Peter, 71–72, 74, 77

Lomandra, 241
  Breeze, 27, 241
Lonicera nitida 'Baggesen's Gold', 211
loquat, 125, 219, 221
  'Champagne', 216
loropetalum, 153, 211, 239, 243
Lotus berthelotii, 231

M

magnolia, 162, 163
  'Little Gem', 164
mandarin citrus, 91
mangave
  'Inkblot', 39
  'Lavender Lady', iv, 174
manzanita (*Arctostaphylos*), 215, 217, 221
maples, 141
marigold, 89, 106, 118, 207
meaningful items, placing, 159
Melianthus major. See honeybush
melon, 97
Mexican weeping bamboo, 215, 223
micro lawns, 211
milkweed, 227
mint, 92, 141, 152
mizuna, 74
mountain cabbage tree (*Cussonia paniculata*), 8, 94
mullein (*Verbascum*), 146, 149
mustard, wild, 218
myoga ginger (*Zingiber mioga*), 217
myrtle (*Myrtus*), 235, 236

N

nandina, 124
nasturtium, 19, 20, 89, 134, 146, 207, 250
Natal plum (*Carissa macrocarpa*), 221, 227, 229
Nelson, Zach, 133, 134, 138
Nepeta, 138
Newton, Fredrika, 150–53, 155–56, 158
New Zealand flax (*Phormium*), 91, 174, 175, 227, 229
New Zealand hair sedge (*Carex testacea*), 55, 59, 71, 177
Nguyen, Sarah, 121, 124
Nicotiana tabacum. See tobacco
Nigella, 181

O

olive, 71, 77, 79, 227, 229, 239, 241
Opuntia. See prickly pear
orange, 114, 245
  'Chinotto', 43, 59, 231
oregano, 68

Osmanthus fragrans, 101, 141
Owens, Linval, 245

P

palm (*Chamaerops*), 239, 241
pansy, 83, 89
Papaver nudicaule. See Iceland poppy
P. somniferum. See breadseed poppy
papyrus, 255
parsley, 68, 218
passion flower (*Passiflora caerulea*), 149
passion fruit, 204, 245, 246, 251, 252
pathways, 26, 199, 243
pea, 16, 72
    'North Shore', 7
    'Triple G', 7
peaches, 152
pear, 113, 127, 177
    'Bartlett', 235
    'Warren', 48
Pelargonium. See scented geranium
penstemon, 129
Penstemon heterophyllus 'Margarita
    BOP', 215, 218
pepper, 92, 97, 225, 231
    shishito, 237
    wiri wiri, 207
perennials, 42–55. *See also individual
    plants*
Perlitch, Sara, 235–39, 241
Perovskia 'Little Spire'. *See* Russian sage
persimmon, 141, 177, 179, 220, 221,
    223, 225, 227, 229
Peruvian lily (*Alstroemeria*), 113, 114,
    127, 129, 153, 158, 169
philodendron, 189, 196
Phormium. See New Zealand flax
Pieris japonica 'Flaming Silver', 191
pincushion flowers (*Scabiosa*), 108, 109
pineapple guava (*Feijoa sellowiana*), 8,
    55, 114, 133, 152, 175, 215, 216,
    219, 227, 231, 239, 241
pineapple quince (*Cydonia oblonga*),
    43, 87
Pine House Edible Gardens, 5, 10
pinks (*Dianthus*), 89, 109, 207, 235
Pittosporum, 41, 173
P. crassifolium 'Compactum', 249
P. tenuifolium 'Marjorie Channon', 8
P. tobira 'Wheeler's Dwarf', 34, 87,
    95, 121
plum, 145, 179
    'Santa Rosa', 202, 235
pluot, 179
    Dapple Dandy, 247
Podocarpus, 127, 183, 188, 196, 245

pomegranate, 71, 72, 225, 229, 231, 249
    'Wonderful', 48
Poon, Andrew, 121, 127
poppy
    breadseed, 8, 20, 99, 138, 141
    California, 55, 71, 215, 218, 221
    Iceland, 20, 141
    'Naughty Nineties', 114
prickly pear (*Opuntia*), 41, 84
protea, 174
pumpkin, 227

Q

Queen of the Night cactus (*Epiphyllum
    oxypetalum*), 77
Quercus agrifolia. See coast live oak
quince, 179

R

raised beds, 19–21, 68
ranunculus, 20, 77
raspberry, 183, 201
red Abyssinian banana (*Ensete
    ventricosum* 'Maurelii'), 196,
    213, 255
rhubarb, 189, 227, 232, 252
Richardson, Verna, 232
rose, 53, 71, 77, 91, 92, 102, 121, 134,
    141, 145, 146, 148, 153, 163, 189,
    195, 227, 231, 235, 252
    Angel Face, 177
    Burgundy Iceberg, 162, 169, 191
    'Distant Drums', 245, 247
    Frida Kahlo, 156
    'Iceberg', 169
    Lady of Shallot, 4
roselle, 13, 207, 246, 251
rosemary, 72, 114, 152, 219, 221
rubber plant, 156
Rubus idaeus 'Heritage'. *See*
    everbearing raspberry
rue, 143
Russian sage (*Perovskia* 'Little
    Spire'), 235

S

sage, 68, 146
    'Berggarten', 68
    golden, 169
    Russian, 235
sago palm, 163
Salvia
    'Indigo Spires', 169
    Love and Wishes, 211
    Mystic Spires Blue, 164, 169, 172,
        181, 196

'Wendy's Wish', 41, 43, 196, 237
Wish series, 129
S. chiapensis, 28, 89
Sambucus nigra spp. *cerulea. See*
    elderberry
sanguisorba, 235
Santa Barbara daisy (*Erigeron*
    karvinskianus), 34, 121, 129
Scabiosa. See pincushion flowers
scented geranium (*Pelargonium*), 4, 8,
    89, 106, 109, 141, 165, 189
sea lavender (*Limonium perezii*), 51, 121
seating, 25, 187
Segre, Marcy and Dave, 163–64,
    166, 169
Senecio cineraria. See dusty miller
S. mandraliscae, 55, 215, 218
sensory gardens, creating, 141
Shackleton, Denise, 225, 229, 231–32
shell ginger (*Alpinia zerumbet*), 28, 245
Sher, Lacey, 59, 60, 63
Sher, Pam, 59–60, 67
shishito pepper, 237
shiso, 67, 83, 237
smoke tree (*Cotinus*), 219, 221
snapdragon, 20, 77, 89, 109, 110
Soja, Charlotte and Jon, 81–82, 84
sorrel, 13, 207, 246, 251
sowthistle, 218
squash, 97, 104, 114, 134, 227, 250
Stachys byzantina. See lamb's ear
starter summer veggie gardens, 96–97
strawberry, 11, 68, 81, 97, 109, 186, 207
Strelitzia nicolai. See giant bird of
    paradise
sun exposure, 16, 19
sunflower, 20, 89, 134, 169
sweet potato (*Ipomoea batatas*), 68, 231
Swiss chard, 97

T

Tanacetum parthenium. See feverfew
tangerines, 121
taro (*Colocasia esculenta*), 172, 175
tarragon, 68
Tetrapanax papyrifer, 231
Teucrium. See germander
Thomas, Rose and Jerry, 181, 183,
    185–86
thyme, 68
    creeping, 123
    lemon, 68
tobacco (*Nicotiana tabacum*), 110,
    143, 146
tomato, 92, 97, 114, 134, 183, 225, 227
    'Sun Gold', 202

toyon (*Heteromeles arbutifolia*), 59
Trachelium caeruleum, 153, 158
    'Hamer Pandora', 4, 8, 41, 249
Trachycarpus fortunei. See windmill palm
tree aloe (*Aloe* 'Hercules'), 215, 219
tree fern, 191, 194
triangulation, 37
tulip, 101
2m Foundation, 133

U

Ugni molinae. See Chilean guava
Umbellularia californica. See
    California bay
umbrella bamboo (*Fargesia*
    murielae), 194
ume (*Prunus mume*), 177, 178

V

veggie gardens, starter summer, 96–97
Verbascum. See mullein
Verbena bonariensis, 11, 55, 114, 215,
    219, 241
V. lilacina 'De La Mina', 218
Veronica, 108
viburnum, 101
vines, 46. *See also individual plants*
viola, 20, 89

W

wallflower (*Erysimum*), 114, 121, 129
wasabi, 237
Watson, Courtney, 143–46, 149
weeping mulberry, 51, 239
white mugwort (*Artemisia lactiflora*), 149
willow, 235, 236
windmill palm (*Trachycarpus fortunei*),
    235, 236
wiri wiri pepper, 207
Wooten, Harold, 91–92

Y

yarrow (*Achillea millefolium*), 4, 118,
    129, 143, 145, 149
    'Cerise Queen', 55
    'Hoffnung', 235
yucca, 27, 165, 245
Yucca recurvifolia, 94
yuzu (*Citrus junos*), 121, 177

Z

Za'atar, 106
Zingiber mioga. See myoga ginger
zinnia, 20, 109, 114, 134, 207
zucchini, 225

Text copyright © 2024 by Leslie Bennett
Photographs copyright © 2024 by Rachel Weill, except as noted below

Photos copyright © 2024 by Caitlin Atkinson: pages 46 (bottom), 55, 58, 61,
64–65, 67 (bottom right), 122–23, 125 (top), 126, 128–29, 135 (bottom left),
137 (right), 214–15, 216 (right), 217–19, 221–22
Photos copyright © 2024 by David Fenton: pages 112, 114 (bottom left),
115 (top left), and 119
Photos copyright © 2024 by Marion Brenner: pages 117 and 118

All rights reserved.
Published in the United States by Ten Speed Press, an imprint of the Crown
Publishing Group, a division of Penguin Random House LLC, New York.
TenSpeed.com

Ten Speed Press and the Ten Speed Press colophon are registered trademarks
of Penguin Random House LLC.

Typefaces: Latinotype's Juana, Latinotype's Texta, and Google's Noto Sans

Library of Congress Cataloging-in-Publication Data
Names: Bennett, Leslie, 1978- author. | Chai, Julie, author. Title: Garden
wonderland : create life-changing outdoor spaces for beauty, harvest,
meaning, and joy / by Leslie Bennett and Julie Chai. Identifiers: LCCN
2023005501 (print) | LCCN 2023005502 (ebook) | ISBN 9781984861382
(hardcover) | ISBN 9781984861399 (ebook) Subjects: LCSH: Gardening.
Classification: LCC SB453 .B4166 2024 (print) | LCC SB453 (ebook) | DDC 635—
dc23/eng/20230711
LC record available at https://lccn.loc.gov/2023005501
LC ebook record available at https://lccn.loc.gov/2023005502

Hardcover ISBN: 978-1-9848-6138-2
eBook ISBN: 978-1-9848-6139-9

Printed in China

Acquiring editor: Lisa Regul | Project editor: Claire Yee
Production editor: Sohayla Farman | Editorial assistant: Gabby Urena
Designer: Ashley Lima | Art director: Betsy Stromberg
Production designers: Mari Gill and Faith Hague
Production manager: Dan Myers | Prepress color manager: Jane Chinn
Copyeditor: Lisa Theobald | Proofreader: Lisa Brousseau
Indexer: Ken DellaPenta
Publicist: Kristin Casemore | Marketer: Joey Lozada

10 9 8 7 6 5 4 3 2 1

First Edition

"Yes, your garden can change your life. Leslie Bennett shows you how to put your heart and muscle into your garden, so that it becomes a source of everything that matters the most. Leslie leads the way toward a garden-centric life that is richer, more delicious, and more connected."

—FLORA GRUBB, owner of Flora Grubb Gardens

"Celebrated landscape designer Leslie Bennett believes that gardens are for all. In *Garden Wonderland* she treats us to an accessible garden-making approach to create our own plant-based spaces that provide sustenance, beauty, and wonder. Follow her journey through the design process and you'll gain more than a pretty landscape—you'll redefine your own relationship with nature."

—DEBRA PRINZING, author of *Where We Bloom* and *Slow Flowers*

"In the world of food gardens, no one compares to Leslie Bennett. Packed with tangible instruction, her new book lets all of us in on her design and production secrets. This book is my new coffee table centerpiece that I'll refer to again and again in my own design work. If you have even a slight desire for a more beautiful and bountiful landscape, this is a must-read that you'll devour in a weekend and then refer back to season after season."

—NICOLE JOHNSEY BURKE, founder of Gardenary Inc. and author of *Kitchen Garden Revival* and *Leaves, Roots & Fruit*